The most effective method to Work From Home and Bring in Cash.

Twenty Tested Home-Based Businesses You Can Start Right Now.

Sam kane

Table of Contents

5. Course online

6.   Web-based   Entertainment   The
executives.
- How to Win at Social Media: A
  Manual   for   Effective
  Administration
- Connecting with Your Crowd
7. Remote helper

Chapter   Three: 13   Demonstrated
Locally   established   Organisations
(Offline).

1. Providing food and Individual Cook
Administrations.

2. Locally established Bread shop or
Candy store.

3.   Specialty   and   craftworker
Merchandise Creation.

4.   Services   for   Childcare   and
Babysitting.

5. Pet sitting and Canine strolling.

6. Home Improvement and Jack of all trades Administrations.

7. Individual Preparation and Wellness Training.

8. Music Illustrations and Mentoring.

9. Occasion Arranging and Party Plan.

10. Locally situated Photography Administrations.

11. Sewing and Changes Administration.

12. Locally situated Magnificence Administrations.

13. Plant Spread and Cultivating Administrations.

Conclusion

Introduction

Welcome to the astonishing universe of telecommuting and building your own business! This introduction will lead you through the fascinating world of home-based businesses and open the door to learning more about the 13 successful businesses you can start today.

The Flourishing Scene of Locally established Organisations:

The computerised upheaval has changed the manner in which we work. Remote positions are soaring, and creative innovation engages people to divert their interests into benefits from the solace of their own homes. The adaptability, control, and pay potential presented by locally situated adventures are charming, filling a flourishing pioneering soul.

Envision a clamouring commercial centre, not one with physical stores, yet a lively computerised and nearby environment overflowing with locally established organisations. This is the truth we live in today, where the pioneering soul has flourished in lounge rooms, spare rooms, and kitchen tables. The ascent of locally established organisations isn't simply a trend; it's an extraordinary change in the manner we work and add to the economy.

We should investigate the key variables powering this blast:

1. Computerised Insurgency: The web and tech progressions have democratised business venture. People can launch online stores, freelance their skills, and connect with clients worldwide without having a physical storefront thanks to platforms like Shopify, Etsy, and Upwork.

2. Remote Work Pattern: The Coronavirus pandemic sped up the acknowledgment of remote work, and many organisations keep on embracing adaptable work plans. This makes it

possible for professionals who work from home to reach a broader clientele.

3. Web based business Blast: Internet shopping has turned into a lifestyle for some, making a gigantic market for locally established organisations offering everything from handcrafted specialties to prepared merchandise to computerised items.

4. Increasing Interest in Personalized Services: Buyers are progressively looking for customised answers for their necessities, setting out open doors for locally established organizations represents considerable authority in specialty administrations like coaching, counseling, and pet consideration.

5. Reduced Initial Costs: With innovation smoothing out undertakings and online stages offering reasonable promoting devices, sending off a locally situated business is frequently more affordable than customary physical endeavors.

The advantages of joining this flourishing scene are various.

Flexibility and balancing work and life: Set up your own schedule, work from anyplace with a web association, and appreciate more prominent command over your timetable.

Seek after Your Interests: Transform your abilities and interests into a satisfying profession and construct a business you're really energetic about.

Work for yourself: acquire freedom and independence, pursue your own choices, and receive the benefits of your persistent effort.

Limitless Pay Potential: Your buying potential isn't restricted to a proper compensation; Your business and income can grow with your hard work and dedication.

Add to the Neighborhood Economy: Home-based businesses add diversity to the economic landscape, support local communities, and create jobs.

This is only the start of our process of investigating the astonishing universe of locally situated organizations. Remain tuned as we dive into the points of interest of 13 demonstrated adventures you can send off today, both on the web and disconnected, and begin fabricating your own locally situated example of overcoming adversity!

Chapter One
Why Start a Locally established Business in 2024?

2024 presents a powerful coincidence of elements making an excellent opportunity to send off a locally situated business. Assuming you're thinking about taking the jump, here are a few convincing justifications for why:

1. The Ascent of Remote Work:

The pandemic pushed organizations to embrace remote work models, and many currently see its advantages. This establishes a strong climate for locally situated adventures, lessening the requirement for actual office space and permitting you to take advantage of a more extensive ability pool.

2. Boom in e-commerce:

Internet shopping proceeds with its flood, with customers progressively going to their PCs and cell phones for everything from food to furniture. This opens up a huge market for computerized retail facades and online administrations, allowing you to arrive at clients across the globe.

3. Tech-Driven Devices:
State-of-the-art innovations like distributed computing, project the board stages, and man-made intelligence fueled promoting instruments make it more straightforward than at any other time to oversee errands, market your business, and arrive at clients. You can maintain a fruitful business from your lounge with the right devices.

4. Increasing Interest in Personalized Services:
Shoppers are progressively looking for customized arrangements and one of a kind encounters. This opens entryways for specialty locally established organizations spend significant time in regions like counseling, training, handcrafted items, and exceptional nearby administrations.

5. Reduced Initial Costs:

Typically, starting a home-based business is less expensive than starting a traditional business because technology simplifies tasks and online platforms offer inexpensive marketing tools. You can avoid the overhead costs of hiring staff and renting office space.

Past these general patterns, 2024 offers a few exceptional benefits:

Expanded center on prosperity: The pandemic has made individuals more aware of their physical and emotional well-being, setting out open doors for organisations offering health items, administrations, and instructing.

Maintainability and eco-awareness: Home-based businesses that are focused on sustainability and ethical practices are opening up because of consumers' growing demand for environmentally friendly goods and services.

Ascent of the maker economy: Stages like YouTube, TikTok, and Instagram are engaging people to fabricate crowds and adapt their substance, setting out thrilling open doors for locally established makers and powerhouses.

Beginning a locally established business in 2024 isn't just about getting away from the workspace; it's tied in with jumping all over the chance to work for yourself, seek after your interests, and add to a flourishing and developing economy.

Prepared to plunge further? Let's look at the 13 tried-and-true home-based businesses you can start today, both online and offline, to help you realize your entrepreneurial ambitions!

• Choosing the Right Business for You.

Choosing the right home-based business in 2024 is an exciting and significant choice for you personally. While the open doors are immense, finding the ideal fit requires contemplation and vital preparation. Here are a few critical variables to consider:

1. Your Abilities and Interests:

What are you great at? Distinguish your regular abilities and bought abilities. Are you an expert baker, an adept coder, or an organized by nature? Using your current abilities will make the expectation to absorb information smoother and increment your odds of coming out on top.

What are you energetic about? Is there a side interest you could transform into a productive endeavor? Energy powers your drive and responsibility, causing extended periods of time to feel less like work and more like an agreeable pursuit.

2. Market Interest:

Does your thought take care of an issue or take care of a need? Research your objective market and recognize existing holes or specialty open doors.

Is there a sufficiently enormous crowd able to pay for your item or administration? Try not to become involved with a craze with restricted life span. Search for patterns with workable development potential.

3. Startup Expenses and Venture:

How much capital might you at any point commit to sending off your business? Be practical about your monetary assets and pick a choice that lines up with your spending plan.

Consider progressing costs like hardware, programming, showcasing, and materials.

4. Time Responsibility:

Speak the truth about how long you can reasonably commit to your business.

Building an effective endeavor requires exertion and devotion. Make sure you can handle the workload by considering your current commitments and schedule.

5. Way of life Inclinations:

Do you appreciate working freely or teaming up with others? A few organisations require negligible collaboration, while others blossom with client connections.

Ponder your optimal workplace. Think about commotion, interruption, and travel engaged with various plans of action.

Keep in mind, there's no one size-fits-all solution to picking the right locally situated business. Take as much time as is needed, investigate your choices, and pay attention to your instinct. The following piece of our process will dig into 13 demonstrated locally established organisations, both on the web and disconnected, offering assorted choices to match your remarkable abilities, interests, and objectives.

Chapter Two
7 Demonstrated Locally established Organizations (On the web).

Welcome to the thrilling universe of online locally situated organizations! This segment will release the capability of the advanced domain, exhibiting 13 demonstrated adventures you can send off from the solace of your own home. Thus, get your PC, release your imagination, and how about we investigate the open doors:

1. E-commerce

Create your very own online storefront! Sell hand tailored merchandise, arranged rare finds, or outsource popular items. Stages like Shopify, Etsy, and Amazon give all that you really want from item postings to arrange satisfaction.

Ok, online business! Building your own advanced customer facing facade is an intriguing and possibly rewarding web-based locally established undertaking. However, exploring the universe of web-based business can be a piece overwhelming, so we should plunge further and disentangle its true capacity! Priorities straight: What do you enjoy selling most?

Made-to-order goods: Could it be said that you are an imaginative soul with a talent for weaving comfortable scarves, preparing flavorful treats, or creating shocking gems? For showcasing your individual creations, e-commerce platforms like Etsy are ideal.

Arranged one of a kind finds: Do you have an insightful eye for unexpected, yet invaluable treasures at swap meets and secondhand shops? By selling curated vintage clothing, furniture, or home decor on platforms like Shopify, you can turn your talent for treasure hunting into a thriving business.

Dropshipping: Maybe you have an eye for moving items yet don't have any desire to manage stock administration. Outsourcing permits you to sell items straightforwardly from a provider to your clients, killing the need to hold stock yourself.

When you have your item specialty as a top priority, we should investigate a few stages to construct your computerised retail facade:

Shopify: a leading e-commerce platform with effective marketing, product, and order management tools. Shopify accompanies different evaluating plans and an extensive variety of additional items to tweak your store.

Etsy: A sanctuary for handmade merchandise, Etsy interfaces you with a huge number of potential clients who esteem extraordinary and craftworker made items. Their charges are low, making it an extraordinary beginning stage for new venders.

Amazon: The online business monster gives huge reach and admittance to a monstrous client base. However, Amazon's fees can be higher than those of other platforms, and competition there can be fierce.

However, more than just a pretty storefront is required to establish a successful e-commerce business.

- **Consider the following key strategies:**

Item photography and portrayals: The key to attracting attention and persuading customers to make a purchase is to use captivating descriptions and high-quality images. Put resources into great item photography and carve out opportunity to compose connecting with portrayals that feature the advantages and elements of your contributions.

Advertising and web-based entertainment: Spread the news about your store! Use web-based entertainment stages like Instagram, Facebook, and Pinterest to feature your items and interface with clients. Paid promoting efforts on these stages can additionally help your scope.

Client support: Give brilliant client care to fabricate trust and reliability. Answer quickly to requests, handle returns and trades proficiently, and put in any amount of work to satisfy your clients.

Online business offers enormous potential for locally established business achievement. Keep in mind that finding your niche, selecting the platform, and creating a compelling brand experience for your customers are the keys. With commitment and the right systems, you can construct a flourishing internet based store from the solace of your own home!

Building a successful e-commerce business causes a delicate balancing act involving several other crucial aspects, besides the fundamental components of your product, platform, and marketing. Here are a few extra perspectives to consider for long haul development and success:

Planned operations and Satisfaction:
Delivery and shipping: Cost, speed, and dependability should all be taken into account when devising your shipping

strategy. Offer cutthroat transportation rates, investigate satisfaction choices like outsourcing or outsider operations (3PL) to smooth out satisfaction, and guarantee clear conveyance timetables to oversee client assumptions.

Stock administration: Keep up with ideal stock levels to stay away from stock-outs or abundance stock. Consistently dissect deals with information, gauge interest, and carry out stock administration instruments to guarantee smooth item stream.

Security and processing of payments:
Consistent checkout experience: Provide a wide range of secure payment options, including e-wallets, credit cards, debit cards, payment gateways, and credit cards, for an easy and convenient checkout process. Build customer trust and ensure that your website is PCI-compliant for secure data handling.

Building a Local area and Brand Steadfastness:

Draw in with your clients: Encourage a feeling of local area and brand steadfastness by offering magnificent client support, answering surveys and input quickly, and running connecting with virtual entertainment missions or faithfulness programs.

Make the experience unique: Execute email showcasing computerization to customise correspondences, suggest important items in view of procurement history, and deal with designated advancements to make clients drew in and want more and more.

Information Examination and Improvement:

Track key measurements: Routinely screen key online business measurements like site traffic, change rates, normal request worth, and client getting cost (CAC) to distinguish regions for development and upgrade your promoting techniques.

A/B testing: try! use A/B testing to improve your site, item depictions, suggestions to take action, and promoting efforts to find what resounds best with your clients.

Compliance with Law and Regulation:

Figure out nearby guidelines: Guarantee your business consents to all significant internet business regulations, item wellbeing guidelines, and assessment prerequisites. Look for proficient exhortation if necessary to explore legalities and keep away from likely traps.

Remaining versatile and future-sealed:

Embrace change: The internet business scene is continually advancing. Remain informed about industry patterns, raising advancements, and changing client inclinations to adjust your business method and stay serious.

Put resources into consistent learning: try not to quit learning! Go to studios, take part in web-based courses, and organise with other online business visionaries to remain on top of things and continually work on your abilities and information.

Keep in mind, fabricating a fruitful internet business is a persistent excursion, not an aim. By focusing on these extra factors close by your center components, you can set your web-based adventure on a way to workable development and long haul thriving.

2. Freelancing

Release your range of abilities! Offer composition, altering, visual communication, web advancement, online entertainment on the board, virtual help, and that's just the beginning. Build your own portfolio and website or connect with clients on platforms like Upwork, Fiverr, and Freelancer.

The freedom to choose your projects, set your own hours, and be your own boss that comes with freelance work is truly alluring. Assuming you're thinking about joining the flourishing universe of internet outsourcing, we should dig further into investigating this intriguing way!

Priorities straight: what abilities and aptitude might you at any point offer?

Composing and altering: Do you employ the force of the pen with accuracy and beauty? Independent composing opens ways to creating convincing articles, site duplicate, showcasing materials, and secretly composing books.

Visual depiction and web advancement: Reinvigorate advanced spaces! Outsourcing in these fields permits you to make dazzling visuals, foster easy-to-use sites, and construct drawing in web-based encounters.

Virtual entertainment the executives: Can you easily get around the constantly changing social media landscape? Assist organizations with making effective virtual entertainment techniques, deal with their internet based presence, and interface with their main interest group.

Virtual help: Turn into the remote right-hand individual! Offer authoritative, specialised, or inventive help to clients, overseeing plans, messages, ventures, and the sky is the limit from there.

The options are endless! Whether you're an information investigator, interpreter, software engineer, picture taker, or have some other significant ability, outsourcing gives a road to adapt your mastery.

Whenever you've distinguished your specialty, investigating these stages can send off your independent process:

Upwork: A worldwide commercial center interfacing specialists with clients across different enterprises. Upwork has a lot of potential projects, secure payment options, and a competitive bidding system.

Fiverr: Known for its miniature undertakings and gigs, Fiverr allows you to offer more modest, obvious administrations at fixed costs. It's great for exhibiting explicit abilities and drawing on new clients rapidly.

Freelancer.com: Like Upwork, Freelancer.com interfaces consultants with clients around the world. Its attention on long haul activities can be appropriate for building enduring associations with clients.

The outcome of outsourcing goes past tracking down a stage.
Here are a few vital procedures to flourish in this cutthroat scene:
Construct areas of strength for a: Feature your best work, feature your abilities and experience, and make an expert portfolio site or online presence.
Foster your valuing technique: Research regular rates in your field, think about your experience and worth, and set cutthroat costs that mirror your aptitude.
Make convincing recommendations: Figure out how to compose a designated proposition that obviously

imparts your worth and persuades clients to pick you.

Convey remarkable help: Go above and beyond for your customers. Fulfill time constraints, convey real, and surpass assumptions to fabricate trust and secure recurrent business.

Market yourself: To keep your pipeline full and attract new clients, build a strong online presence, and establish a network of other freelancers.
Outsourcing offers enormous potential for money and autonomy. Keep in mind that building a successful freelance career takes time, commitment, and ongoing education. By leveling up your abilities, making areas of strength for a, and conveying uncommon help, you can explore the universe of outsourcing with certainty and cut your own way to progress.

Deciphering the Outsourcing Code: Building a Flourishing Business

The charm of outsourcing - limitless opportunity, self-assurance, and limitless pay potential - is obvious. However, more than just expertise and enthusiasm are required to navigate this exciting landscape. Consider the following essential pillars of success if you want to truly transform your freelance dreams into a thriving business.

Cementing Your Establishment:

Hone your specialty: Rather than being a handyman, ace a particular expertise or industry. This permits you to order higher rates, draw in ideal clients, and stand apart from the group.

Create a convincing portfolio: Feature your best work in a manner that resounds with your interest group. Put resources into an expert site or online portfolio stage to show your abilities and experience, really.

Recognize your worth: Research industry rates, think about your skill and experience, and with certainty set serious costs that mirror your worth. Try not to underestimate your administrations!

Building Your Client Base:
Network like an ace: Connect with other freelancers and potential clients both online and offline, attend industry events, and cultivate genuine relationships. Verbal references are gold in the independent world.

Influence online stages: Make use of platforms like Upwork, Fiverr, and Freelancer to reach new customers and broaden your reach. Don't depend only on them; expand your advertising channels.

Make an overpowering proposition: Figure out how to compose drawing recommendations that feature your exceptional offer and persuade clients to pick you over the opposition. Center on their necessities and how you can tackle their concerns.

Conveying First class Administration:
The key is communication: Keep up with clear and steady correspondence with clients throughout the undertaking. Set assumptions, update them routinely, and be effectively reachable. Address concerns proactively and promptly in response to inquiries.

Surpass assumptions: Try not to simply comply with time constraints; convey extraordinary outcomes that surpass client assumptions. This goes far in building trust and getting rehash business.

Be flexible and proactive: Embrace input, be available to modifications, and remain adaptable to oblige client needs. This shows incredible skill and a guarantee of their prosperity.

Showcasing Yourself for Long haul Achievement:
Construct major areas of strength for a brand: Characterise your image voice, make a predictable web-based presence (site, online entertainment profiles), and effectively draw in with your crowd. Share important substance, exhibit your skill, and interface on an individual level.

Put resources into nonstop learning: The independent world is continually advancing. To remain competitive and provide even more value to your customers, attend workshops and courses, keep up with industry trends, and improve your skills.

Examine and adjust: Analyze your outcomes, track your progress, and monitor important metrics like client acquisition cost, project turnaround time, and client satisfaction. Use information to recognize regions for development and refine your procedures for long haul achievement.

Keep in mind, constructing a flourishing independent business takes time, commitment, and diligence. Try not to get put by introductory difficulties down; use them as learning open doors and continue to refine your method. You can achieve freedom as a freelancer and financial independence with a solid foundation, effective marketing, and exceptional client service.

Is there a particular part of your independent process to dive further into? Perhaps you are having trouble creating compelling proposals or setting up your online presence. I'm here to help you along the way in your freelance career!

3. Blogs and video blogs.

Share your insight and associate with a crowd of people! Compose enlightening blog entries, make connecting with video blogs, or send off a digital recording. Adapt your substance through publicising, partner promoting, and selling your own items and courses.

Publishing content to a blog and Vlogging: Sharing Your Voice and Building a Group of people
Welcome to the charming universe of writing for a blog and vlogging, where you can share your interests, interface with a group of people, and even form a web-based business! However, before you plunge headfirst into this exciting realm, let's investigate the specifics of each platform to determine which one is most appropriate for your voice and:
:
The composed word becomes the dominant focal point: make connecting

with articles, share educational instructional exercises, or weave enthralling stories in blog entries. Offer your viewpoints, dig into your skill, and construct a local area around your composed substance.

Adaptability in design: Try different things with various styles, from long-structure articles to scaled down, inject personality, humor, or insightful analysis into your writing.

Openness at its best: Contact a worldwide crowd with an insignificant venture. Begin your blog with promptly accessible stages like WordPress or Blogger and effectively share your substance across web-based.

Vlogging:

Release the force of video: Catch your crowd's consideration with dynamic visuals, drawing in narrating, and your own alluring character. Video blogs can cover anything from make a trip experiences to cooking instructional exercises to inside and out item surveys.

Building a nearer association: The visual and hear-able components of video blogs encourage a more grounded close to home association with your crowd. You can show your sincerity, convey your feelings, and form a more intimate connection with your viewers.

Higher boundaries to passage: Requires gear like cameras, mouthpieces, and altering programming. Vlogging also requires strong video editing skills and a confident presence in front of the camera.

Presently, how would you pick the ideal stage for you? Think about these variables:

Your usual range of familiarity: Do you prefer to share your personality through video or through writing? Pick the configuration that permits you to be your valid and drawing in self.

Your interest group: Who would you like to reach? Research your crowd's favored substance utilization propensities and pick the stage where they're dynamic.

Your accessible assets: Vlogging requires a larger initial investment in equipment and editing software. Blogging has a lower barrier to entry. When deciding, consider your financial resources and your technical abilities.

Recall, the outcome in both contributing to a blog and vlogging lies past picking the right stage:

Quality written substance is the final deciding factor (or sovereign!): Whether you compose or film, focus on top-notch content that teaches, engages, or moves your crowd. Center on offering worth and building a certified association.

Consistency is vital: Customary posting is critical for building a faithful following. Foster a substance schedule, put forth sensible objectives, and focus on appearing for your crowd reliably.

Commitment matters: Try not to simply communicate, collaborate! Answer remarks, answer questions, and take part in web-based conversations. Create a sense of community around your content and give your audience a sense of worth.

Publishing content to a blog and vlogging offer fabulous chances to share your voice, fabricate a brand, and even produce pay. By picking the right stage, making convincing substance, and reliably captivating with your crowd, you can transform your interests into a flourishing web-based adventure.

The Start of Your Dream: A Manual for Fruitful Writing for a blog and Vlogging

The excitement of sharing your voice, interfacing with a group of people, and building a flourishing web-based presence - that is the wizardry of contributing to a blog and vlogging. However, more than just enthusiasm is required to successfully navigate the initial steps. For a deeper look at achieving your goals and dominating the digital space, consider:

Establishing the Groundwork:
Tracking down your specialty: Try not to be a handyman! Distinguish a particular theme or specialized topic that starts your enthusiasm and resounds with your main interest group. This attracts a devoted following and establishes a focused identity.
Making your image: Characterize your voice, your visual style, and your general message. Make a brand character that is predictable across your foundation and reverberates with your interest group.
Picking your foundation: For writing for a blog, investigate easy-to-understand stages like WordPress, Blogger, or Squarespace. For vlogging, choices like YouTube, Vimeo, or even Instagram Reels offer different reach and crowd socioeconomics. Consider your

substance style and ideal interest group while picking.

Building Convincing Substance:

Higher expectations when in doubt: Engaging, well-researched, and informative content should take precedence over frequent posts that are rushed. Offer experiences, recount stories, and offer some benefit to your crowd.

Understand your listeners' perspective: Make your content relevant to their preferences, requirements, and interests. Answer remarks, answer questions, and effectively take part in discussions to fabricate a two-way discourse.

Try to refine: Make it a point to attempt various organizations, styles, and themes. Dissect your crowd commitment and refine your method in view of information and criticism.

Optimizing for expansion:

Search engine optimization for bloggers: Research applicable watchwords and advance your blog entries with legitimate title labels, meta portrayals, and inner connecting. This builds your substance's perceivable in web search tool results.

Thumbnails and titles for vloggers: Make eye-getting thumbnails and convincing titles that arouse watchers' curiosity and support clicks. Use watchwords in your titles for discoverability.

Making use of your content: Share your posts and recordings across web-based entertainment stages, take part in web-based networks, and team up with different makers to contact a more extensive crowd.

Adaptation Systems:
Advertising: Whenever you've constructed a dedicated crowd, consider showing promotions on your blog or

YouTube channel. Research promotion organizations and pick those that line up with your substance and brand.

Offshoot showcasing: Advance pertinent items or administrations through associate connections and buy commissions for bugs made through your suggestions.

Supported content: Join forces with brands to make supported posts or recordings that line up with your specialty and values. For ethical partnerships, ensure disclosure and transparency.

Keep in mind, progress in contributing to a blog and vlogging requires devotion, persistence, and reliable exertion:

Remaining predictable: Foster a substance schedule and stick to it. Posting frequently builds anticipation and maintains audience interest.

Putting resources into learning: Learn video editing and production techniques for vlogging or hone your writing and editing skills for blogging. Persistent learning keeps your substance new and proficient.

Adjusting and developing: Remain refreshed on industry patterns, investigate your presentation, and adjust your procedures considering crowd criticism and information experiences.

The potential outcomes in writing for a blog and vlogging are unending. By building areas of strength for a making great substance, effectively captivating with your crowd, and investigating adaptation open doors, you can transform your enthusiasm into a flourishing web-based adventure.

Do you have a particular part of your writing for a blog or a vlogging venture to investigate further? Maybe you're battling with watchword exploration or video altering procedures. I'm here to be your steady aide throughout your inventive excursion!

Diving Further: Catchphrase Exploration and Video Altering Authority

In our past conversations, we uncovered the astonishing universes of contributing to a blog, vlogging, and their gigantic potential. Presently, we should focus in on two vital viewpoints for augmenting your prosperity: catchphrase exploration and video altering!

Catchphrase Exploration:

Uncovering a treasure map that will lead to engage audiences is like finding the right keywords. This is the way to explore this fundamental angle:

Grasping your crowd: Understand what themes they're looking for and what questions they have. Use apparatuses like Google Patterns, virtual entertainment listening stages, and crowd overviews to grasp their inclinations and language.

Watchword research apparatuses: Influence the force of devices like Google Catchphrase Organizer, Ah refs, and SEMrush. These stages uncover search volume, rivalry, and related catchphrases, assisting you with distinguishing rewarding objective terms.

Long-tail catchphrases: Avoid focusing solely on generic terms; investigate long-tail catchphrases - more unambiguous expressions with lower rivalry yet high buy purpose. These can draw in designated rush hour gridlock and further develop transformation rates.

Integrate catchphrases normally: Don't watchword stuff; coordinate them flawlessly into your substance titles, headings, and body text. Focus on client experience and comprehensibility while decisively putting applicable catchphrases.
Video Altering:
Changing crude film into cleaned show-stoppers is a craftsmanship, and video

altering abilities are indispensable for spellbinding your crowd. Here are a vital stages to alter like an ace:

Narrating structure: Sort out your recording, plan a story stream, and make a convincing start, center, and end. Use changes, cuts, and impacts to direct watchers through your story.

Visual effect: Add visually appealing elements to your video. Use clear shots, various points, and variety revision to keep watchers locked in. For emphasis, think about including text overlays, graphics, and animations.

Sound design and audio: Try not to misjudge the force of sound! Add music, audio effects, and voiceovers to make a vivid encounter. Balance volume levels and guarantee clear perceptibility.

Altering programming: Software for mastering editing, such as DaVinci Resolve, Final Cut Pro, or Adobe

Premiere Pro. Learn fundamental cuts, changes, variety amendment, and sound altering procedures to rejuvenate your vision.

Keep in mind, both watchword examination and video altering are persistent learning ventures:
Remain refreshed: Recent fads and apparatuses arise continually. Investigate online instructional exercises, go to studios, and remain informed about the most recent advancements in Web optimization and video altering to further develop your abilities continually.

Explore and refine: try different things with various methodologies and procedures. Break down your outcomes, track crowd commitment, and refine your procedures, considering what turns out best for yourself as well as your crowd.

Look for input: Share your work with confided in companions, associates, or online networks for valuable analysis. Criticism can assist you with distinguishing regions for development and lift your substance to a higher level.

By becoming amazing at catchphrase examination and video altering, you open the genuine capability of your publishing content to a blog and vlogging tries. Whether you're winding around enrapturing stories on your blog or making outwardly staggering video blogs, these abilities prepare you to draw in the right crowd, connect with them profoundly, and fabricate a flourishing web-based presence.

4. Internet Training and Counseling:

Guide others to progress! Share your mastery in business, life training, wellness, or some other space through web-based instructing and counseling meetings. Use video conferencing stages and internet booking instruments to all around the world arrive at clients.

Directing Others to Progress: Web based Training and Counseling

The charm of sharing your skill, directing others to accomplish their objectives, and building a satisfying internet based business makes web-based training and counseling so dazzling. In this thrilling domain, you influence your insight and experience to engage people and organizations, all from the solace of your own computerized space. However, this course of action causes careful preparation and perseverance. We should plunge further into the basics!

Finding Your Passion:

Recognize your aptitude: What are you truly skilled in and passionate about? Do you succeed in business method, life instructing, wellness preparing, or a particular specialized field? Center on an area where you can really direct others and have a massive effect.

Characterize your optimal client: Who would you like to help? Understanding your interest group's necessities, difficulties, and desires is critical for fitting your instructing or counseling administrations to their particular prerequisites.

Building Your Presence:

Create a memorable brand: Foster an expert site or online stage that exhibits your skill, tributes, and training contributions. Make a brand character that resounds with your main interest group and constructs trust.

Use web-based entertainment: Effectively connect on important stages, share significant substance, and interface with expected clients. Have online courses, lead live back-and-forth discussions, and partake in web-based networks to lay out your position and draw in interest.

Content showcasing: Compose blog entries, make enlightening recordings, or send off digital broadcasts that show your insight and give significant experiences to your crowd. Position yourself as an idea chief in your specialty.

Conveying Outstanding Help:
Customized instructing: Tailor your way of dealing with every client's special requirements and objectives. Foster tweaked training plans, give standard criticism, and proposition progressing support throughout their excursion.

Viable correspondence: Keep up with clear and steady correspondence with your clients. Effectively pay attention to their interests, answer questions instantly, and give useful criticism. Fabricate trust and guarantee a positive instructing experience.

Results-arranged approach: Center on assisting your clients with accomplishing their ideal results. Put forth quantifiable objectives, track progress, and celebrate achievements together. Loyalty and positive word-of-mouth referrals are cultivated when you show your value.

Adapting Your Ability:
Offer a bundle of services: Create various coaching packages with varying prices and support levels. Offer individual meetings, bunch instructing programs, or online courses to take care of different requirements and financial plans.

Make use of booking websites: Make planning and arrangement the board consistent for both you and your clients. Investigate stages like Sharpness Planning or Calendly to smooth out your appointments and installment processes.

Investigate extra income streams: Consider offering digital books, downloadable assets, or online studios close by your instructing administrations. Stability in your finances and the potential for growth can be achieved through income diversification.

Keep in mind that starting a profitable online coaching or consulting business takes time and effort.

Continuous education: Remain refreshed on industry patterns, go to studios, and put resources into proficient advancement to refine your abilities and information. The instructing scene is continually advancing, so continue to figure out how to stay serious.

Organization and construct connections: Interface with different mentors, industry specialists, and expected teammates. Building major areas of strength for a can open ways to new open doors and extend your span.

Accept feedback and adjust: Break down your outcomes, accumulate client criticism, and adjust your method considering what's functioning admirably and what could be gotten to the next level. Adaptability and spryness are vital to long haul achievement.

Web based training and counseling offer colossal potential for individual satisfaction and monetary prizes. You can turn your expertise into a thriving online business and empower others to achieve their goals by identifying your niche, developing a robust online presence, providing exceptional service, and evaluating appropriate monetization strategies.

From a Vision to a Reality: Sending off a Flourishing Web based Training and Counseling Business

The way to outcome in web-based training and counseling is cleared with enthusiasm, ability, and vital execution. We should dig further into the commonsense advances that will direct you from an introductory plan to a thriving internet based business:

Establishing the Groundwork:

Refine your specialty: Try not to be a handyman! Limited down your concentration to a particular subject where you succeed and really reverberate with your optimal client. This considers further effect and draws in a designated crowd.

Create a profile of your ideal client: Comprehend your interest group's socioeconomics, difficulties, goals, and online way of behaving. Research their favored correspondence channels and designed your way to deal with interface successfully.

Foster your training philosophy: Characterize your novel training system or procedure. How will you help your customers reach their objectives?

What devices, methods, and assets will you influence?
Building your internet based presence:
Make an expert site: Your online storefront is your website. Put resources into an easy-to-understand stage that features your skill, tributes, training bundles, and booking choices. Guarantee clear route and portable responsiveness.
Use virtual entertainment decisively: Pick stages where your ideal client invests energy and effectively draws in with them. Share significant substance, answer questions, have live meetings,

and construct a local area around your instructing administrations.

Content promoting is vital: Compose blog entries, make enlightening recordings, or send off a digital broadcast to lie down a good foundation for yourself as an idea chief in your specialty. Offer important experiences, tips, and systems that show your insight and draw in clients.

Coaching that has a transformative effect:

Customize your method: Every client is interesting. Foster redid training plans considering their singular requirements, objectives, and learning styles. Provide session formats that are adaptable to different preferences, such as one-on-one coaching, group coaching, and online courses.

It is essential to communicate effectively: effectively stand by listening to your clients, pose astute inquiries, and give clear, productive input. Keep up with open correspondence channels and fabricate a believing relationship based on common regard.

Focus on outcomes: Assist your clients with laying out quantifiable objectives and keep tabs on their development routinely. Celebrate achievements, offer continuous help, and guarantee they accomplish practical outcomes that go past the instructing meetings.

Expanding your gaining potential:
Create a variety of training programs: Provide tiered packages with varying prices, session frequency, and levels of support. Give choices to frugal clients and very good quality, customized instructing encounters.

Investigate extra income streams: Along with your coaching services, consider offering e-books, resources that can be downloaded, online workshops, or even live retreats. Enhancement can prompt monetary security and development.

Influence online stages: Use arrangement planning and installment handling stages like Keenness Planning or Calendly to smooth out booking and improve on exchanges for both you and your clients.

Ceaselessly refining your excursion:

Invest in your professional growth: The training scene is continually developing. Go to studios, online courses, and organization with different mentors to remain refreshed on industry drifts and refine your abilities.

Look for criticism and adjust: Analyze your outcomes and solicit client feedback. Recognize regions for development and adjust your instructing techniques, promoting methodologies, and administration contributions considering genuine information.

Construct a steady organization: Associate with different mentors, industry specialists, and partners. Sharing resources, experiences, and knowledge can lead to new opportunities and help your business grow.

Keep in mind, constructing a fruitful web-based training and counseling business requires devotion, diligence, and an unfaltering obligation to your clients' prosperity. By putting resources into the right groundwork, conveying excellent help, and consistently adjusting your method, you can direct others to accomplish their objectives and transform your energy into a flourishing web-based adventure.

I have confidence in your capability to move and engage others through your web-based training and counseling business. With the right direction and steady commitment, you can make a satisfying profession and have a certifiable effect on the existences of your clients.

5. Course online

Create your own insight foundation! Make and sell online seminars on your own site or stages like Udemy and Skillshare. Show important abilities, share your interests, and produce recurring, automated revenue while enabling others.

 online courses! The web's mother lode of information is simply ready to be shared and eaten up. Whether you're a carefully prepared master longing to grant your insight or a maturing devotee anxious to cut your specialty, online courses offer a thrilling stage to interface with students and construct a flourishing internet based business. However, it's difficult to navigate the world of online course creation. Let's investigate further and unravel the complexities, transforming your knowledge into engaging educational experiences!

Figuring out the Code: Bit by bit Manual for Online Course Achievement

The charm of sharing your insight, influencing lives, and building a worthwhile web-based business through internet-based courses is obvious. However, making an interpretation of a dream into reality requires a reasonable guide and vital execution. We should set out on a bit by bit excursion to change your mastery of an enrapturing opportunity for growth and a flourishing internet based adventure:

1. Tracking down Your Brilliant Specialty:

Energy fills fire: Distinguish a point you're profoundly energetic about - an expertise you've dominated, a field you're continually learning in. Your enthusiasm, which will resonate with them, will intrigue students.

Statistical surveying for progress: Don't just follow the trends; conduct market research as well. Dissect student needs,

contended contributions, and distinguish information holes you can load up with your interesting viewpoint and mastery.
Hone your concentration: While wide points can draw in a bigger crowd, specialty courses frequently order higher charges and cultivate further commitment. Focus on a particular part of your picked field to stick out and take special care of a devoted student base.

2. Creating Convincing Substance:
Structure for dominance: Carefully plan the structure of your course. Partition content into absorbable modules with clear learning targets and drawing in exercises. Guarantee is a coherent stream that keeps understudies pushing ahead with reason.
Assortment keeps them snared: Try not to simply address! Separate text with video illustrations, intelligent tests, downloadable assets, and cooperative undertakings. Take special care of

various learning styles and make the excursion invigorating.

Quality writing is everything: focus on exactness, profundity, and lucidity in your materials. Put resources into altering and creation to guarantee a cleaned and connecting with opportunity for growth. Visuals, sound quality, and content composing all add to proficient conveyance.

3. Building Your Learning Center point:
Strength of the platform: Pick the right stage to have your course. Investigate well known choices like Udemy, Coursera, Workable, or Thinkific. Consider factors like course facilitating highlights, understudy the executives apparatuses, showcasing abilities, and evaluating structures.

Greeting page that believers: Create a landing page for your course that is both user-friendly and visually appealing. Feature key learning results, grandstand understudy tributes, and deal convincing reviews to draw in expected students. Enhance for web indexes and clear route.

Make use of marketing magic. Reach your target audience by utilizing online advertising, influenced partnerships, email marketing, and social media. Create a comprehensive marketing plan to promote your course and encourage enrollment.

4. Connecting with Your Understudies:

Community promotes development: Make a stage for understudies to interface and collaborate, whether through web-based gatherings, conversation sheets, or live interactive discussions. Building a steady local area improves commitment, works with peer learning, and lifts maintenance.

Individualized feedback is important: try not to be an unremarkable teacher! Offer customized criticism on tasks, answer questions expeditiously, and take part in significant discourse with your understudies. Show them you care about their learning process and individual advancement.

Be relevant and up to date: Consistently refine your course happily. Address industry changes, integrate new bits of knowledge, and deal with extra materials to make your understudies connected with and want more and more. Show them that the course is a resource that is always changing.

5. Adapting Your Aptitude:

Evaluating that resounds: Explore different avenues regarding different valuing models. Consider onetime buys, membership charges, or layered evaluating in light obviously includes. Find the sweet spot for your audience and value proposition by analyzing market trends and the offerings of rivals. Groups for esteem: Offer course packages or join your contribution with reciprocal assets like digital books, layouts, or admittance to elite networks to add esteem and boost buys. Give an all-encompassing opportunity for growth.

Past the course: Investigate extra income streams. Consider offering strengthening types of help like one-on-one instructing, live studios, or counseling amazing open doors to your course graduates. Diversification can help you build your expertise and make more money.

Keep in mind, Rome wasn't implicit a day: Building an effective internet based course requires devotion, nonstop improvement, and an enthusiasm for interfacing with students. By following these means, picking the right instruments, and remaining focused on your understudies' prosperity, you can change your insight into a flourishing internet based business and enable people to accomplish their objectives through your enamoring growth opportunity.

I put stock in your capability to rouse and engage students through your web-based course. With the right direction and steadfast devotion, you can turn into a reference point of information in the computerized world, molding the eventual fate of schooling for each understudy!

6. Web-based Entertainment The executives.

Plan brand presence! Assist organizations with dealing with their virtual entertainment accounts by making drawing in happy, booking posts, and drawing in with devotees. Stages like Hootsuite and Cradle can smooth out your work process.

How to Win at Social Media: A Manual for Effective Administration

The steadily developing universe of virtual entertainment offers a dynamic and strong stage for organizations and people to interface with their crowd, fabricate brand mindfulness, and drive commitment. Exploring this complex scene requires key preparation and capable execution. How about we dive into the complexities of virtual entertainment the executives and outfit you with the devices and experiences to accomplish your internet based objectives:

Characterizing Your Online Entertainment Mission:

Choosing your objectives: What are your goals for using social media for? increased community development, increased website traffic, or brand awareness? Obviously, characterize your goals to direct your procedure and measure achievement.

Grasping your audience members' viewpoint: Who are you endeavoring to reach? Understanding your ideal interest group's socioeconomics, interests, and online way of behaving is significant for making pertinent substance and picking the right stages.

How to choose your battlegrounds: Not all stages are made equivalent. Examine where your interest group invests their energy on the web and spotlight on the stages applicable to your objectives and brand character.

Creating Convincing Substance:
Broaden your substance to keep your crowd locked in. Use engaging videos, eye-catching images, informative text, and interactive elements like polls and quizzes.

Narrating becomes the overwhelming focus: Include stories in your content. Share appealing stories, exhibit in the background impressions, and feature client encounters to associate with your crowd on a profound level.

Validness resounds: Be consistent with your image voice and character. Allow your exceptional voice to radiate through your substance and encourage authentic associations with your devotees.

- **Connecting with Your Crowd**

Conversations as opposed to speeches: Online entertainment is a two-way road. Take part in relevant online conversations, respond promptly to comments and messages, and encourage open dialogue with your audience.

Building community is important: Encourage a feeling of the local area around your image. To create a space where your audience feels valued and connected, hold giveaways, live Q&A session, and encourage user-generated content.

Remain important and opportune: Keep your finger on the beat of the latest things and industry news. To connect with your audience on a deeper level, take part in relevant online conversations, respond to topics that are trending, and make use of real-time events.

Analyzing and Keeping Track of Performance:

Information is your companion: Use examination instruments given by every stage to follow key measurements like reach, commitment, and site traffic. Regularly examine your data to determine what is working and what needs to be improved.

Adjust and enhance: Go ahead and investigation and attempt new things. In view of your information bits of knowledge, refine your substance system, change your posting timetable, and test various arrangements to improve your exhibition.

Consistent learning is critical: The virtual entertainment scene is continually developing. Keep up with the latest trends, platforms, and best practices to keep your strategies engaging and effective.

Keep in mind, fruitful web-based entertainment. The board is a long distance race, not a run:

The key is dedication and consistency: Routinely make and offer excellent substance, effectively draw in with your crowd, and reliably dissect your outcomes. Time and effort are required to cultivate a devoted following.

Embrace joint effort: Cooperate with powerhouses in your specialty, team up with different brands for cross-advancement, and take part in important web-based networks to extend your venture and tap into new crowds.

Continuously be learning: Remain on top of things by going to studios, online courses, and industry occasions. Navigating the ever-evolving social media landscape causes continual education and adaptation.

By following these means and zeroing in on making major areas of strength for a character, creating connecting with content, sustaining your crowd, and examining your presentation, you can open the tremendous capability of virtual entertainment and accomplish your web-based objectives. Social media provides an exciting platform for connecting with your audience, developing a thriving online presence, and making a lasting impact, whether you are a seasoned marketer or just starting out.

Together, we should wind around your image story through the embroidery of virtual entertainment and make a dynamic internet based presence that reverberates with your crowd and energizes your prosperity.

Fantastic! We should focus in on unambiguous parts of your virtual entertainment the executives excursion and assist you with making enduring progress. To give the most significant subtleties, might you at any point let me know what region zero in on?

There are a few choices:

1. Content System:

Creating content points of support: Recognizing center subjects and points that resound with your crowd and brand personality.

Content schedule creation: Arranging a timetable for various sorts of content (text, pictures, recordings) and adjusting it to significant occasions, occasions, and patterns.

Improving for various stages: fitting substance configurations and styles for Instagram, Twitter, Facebook, LinkedIn, and so on., to expand commitment on every stage.

2. Commitment and Local area Building:

Inventive ways of starting discussions: encouraging audience participation through live streams, contests, Q&A session, and polls.

establishing authentic relationships: Answering remarks and messages immediately, tending to worries effectively, and commending client created content.

Taking care of and developing your community: Organizing events online, forming exclusive groups, and fostering a sense of community among your followers are all important.

3. Examination and Improvement:
Grasping key measurements: Breaking down information like reach, commitment rate, site traffic, and changes to gauge the adequacy of your method.

Putting forth Shrewd objectives: Characterizing explicit, quantifiable, workable, pertinent, and time-bound objectives to keep tabs on your development and guarantee your endeavors are lined up with your goals.

A/B testing and trial and error: Attempting different substance types, posting times, and commitment procedures to see what reverberates best with your crowd and advance your method.

4. Remaining On the ball:
Staying aware of patterns: Observing industry news, raising stages, and new highlights to adjust your system and remain significant.

The following are competitors and influencers: Gaining from effective online entertainment accounts in your specialty and breaking down their substance and commitment methodologies.

Putting resources into your abilities: Going to studios, online courses, and industry occasions to further develop your virtual entertainment, the executives information and ability ceaselessly.

5. Extra Regions:

Partnerships and Collaboration: Expanding your audience and reach by collaborating with influencers, complementary brands, and relevant communities

Paid Promoting: Investigating likely roads for paid virtual entertainment promoting to target explicit socioeconomics and interests.

Planning and Asset The board: Assigning assets really and tracking down savvy instruments to deal with your virtual entertainment presence.

Keep in mind that achieving success on social media requires ongoing education. You can build a successful online presence, connect with your audience in meaningful ways, and achieve your goals by concentrating on relevant areas, employing strategic strategies, and remaining adaptable.

I'm here to be your strong aide constantly! Let's work together to realize the full potential of social media for your personal or business goals.

7. Remote helper:

Be the remote right-hand individual! Give authoritative, specialized, or inventive help to clients from a distance. Oversee plans, email correspondence, project undertakings, and that's only the tip of the iceberg, offering priceless help to occupied experts.

Exploring the Universe of Virtual Help: Your Guide to Progress
The domain of virtual help offers a dynamic and satisfying vocation way, permitting you to use your abilities and mastery to remotely uphold people and organizations. However, exploring this interesting scene can appear to be overwhelming. That is where I come in, your dependable manual for progress in the menial helper world!
Creating Your Optimal Specialty:
Find your assets: Recognize the abilities and aptitude you succeed at, be it

managerial undertakings, composing, virtual entertainment the executives, or specialized abilities. Play to your normal assets for greatest satisfaction and achievement.

Know your main interest group: Research possible clients, whether solopreneurs, independent ventures, or explicit businesses. Comprehend their necessities and problem areas to as needs be tailor your administrations.

Characterize your exceptional incentive: What separates you from other remote helpers? Feature your specialty aptitude, exceptional abilities, or customized way to deal with draw in your optimal clients.

Creating Your Online Toolbox:

Put resources into fundamental instruments: Furnish yourself with programming and stages that smooth out your work, similar to project the executives' devices, correspondence applications, record editors, and internet planning stages.

Remain well informed: Constantly learn new instruments and innovations pertinent to your specialty. Remain on top of things to offer significant administrations and oversee undertakings proficiently.

Level up your delicate abilities: Correspondence, using time effectively, association, and flexibility are basic. Level up these abilities to succeed in remote work and construct solid client connections.

Tracking down Your Clients:

Create a convincing web-based presence: Foster an expert site or online portfolio displaying your abilities, experience, and tributes. Make it simple for expected clients to find and reach you.

Use online stages: Influence independent commercial centers like Upwork, Fiverr, or Master to associate with clients looking for menial helper administrations. Apply for applicable activities.

Organization and construct connections: Associate with other menial helpers, join online networks, and go to industry occasions. Your organization can open ways to new open doors and references.

Conveying Remarkable help:
Dynamic openness is absolutely vital: Communicate clearly and consistently with your customers. Keep them refreshed in progress, address concerns immediately, and construct trust through straightforwardness.

Proactive and mindful: Before the customer asks, anticipate their needs and provide solutions. Recommend thoughts and improving your errands to amplify esteem conveyed.

Be professional at all times: Maintain elevated expectations of hard working attitude, comply with time constraints reliably, and convey flawless outcomes. Establish a reputation for excellence and dependability.

Streamlining Your Menial helper Excursion:

Put resources into a proficient turn of events: Persistently update your abilities by going to online courses, studios, or confirmations applicable to your picked specialty.

Differentiate your revenue_ sources: Think about offering a variety of services as your virtual assistant. Investigate related contributions like substance creation, accounting, or web-based showcasing to take special care of more extensive client needs.

Put down stopping points and keep up with balance: Working remotely requires discipline. Set clear work hours, lay out limits, and focus on your prosperity to stay balanced and guarantee maintainable achievement.

Keep in mind, fabricating a flourishing remote helper vocation takes time and commitment:

Accept continuous education: The menial helper scene is continually developing. Remain refreshed on industry patterns, adjust your range of abilities, and learn constantly to stay serious.

Look for criticism and move along: Effectively look for criticism from clients and associates. Break down your outcomes, distinguish regions for development, and refine your method by considering genuine information.

Organization and fabricate a strong local area: Associate with other menial helpers, share encounters, and gain from one another. Growth and motivation can both benefit from having a network of support.

I have faith in your ability to succeed as a virtual assistant. You can build a career that is both satisfying and lucrative on your terms by figuring out your niche, expanding your skill set, providing exceptional service, and always learning new things.

Together, we should change your abilities and interests into a flourishing menial helper vocation and enable you to accomplish your expert objectives!

From Competitor to Expert: Profound Jump into Fruitful Virtual Help

You've communicated interest in digging further into the thrilling universe of virtual help! Let's look at specific aspects of your journey with a magnifying glass and show you the way to success. To best offer accommodating subtleties, let me know which region zero in on? Here are a few choices:

1. Finding Your Ideal Market:

Abilities Stock: Assess your assets and experience. Could it be said that you are a genius with association, a scribe professional, or an online entertainment maestro? Recognizing your normal gifts is critical to tracking down a satisfying and beneficial specialty.

Statistical surveying: Investigate different menial helper specialties - authoritative help, specialized help, innovative administrations, and so on. Break down potential client needs and examination current industry patterns to find specialties with appeal major areas of strength for and potential.

Remarkable Selling Recommendation: What sets you apart from the competition? Do you offer specific abilities, a particular language familiarity, or an excellent comprehension of a specific industry? Create an extraordinary incentive that resounds with your interest group.

2. Building Your Arsenal of Virtual Assistants:

Fundamental Instruments: use tools for project management, communication apps, document editors, online scheduling platforms, and even time-tracking applications to streamline your work. Put resources into assets that support your effectiveness and efficiency.

Well informed Superhuman: Remain on the ball by finding out about new innovations and instruments pertinent to your specialty. Whether it's dominating a CRM framework or learning progressed virtual entertainment booking stages, ceaseless learning is pivotal for offering state-of-the-art administrations.

Delicate Abilities Authority: Improve your capacity for adaptability, organization, communication, and time management. These are the foundations of fruitful virtual help. Dominating them guarantees consistent client cooperations and proficient work conveyance.

3. Getting in touch with Your Clients:

Online Presence Force to be reckoned with: Foster an expert site or online portfolio exhibiting your abilities, experience, and client tributes. Make it effectively discoverable through web crawlers and streamlined for client transformation.

Independent Commercial center Wizardry: Influence stages like Upwork, Fiverr, or Master to interface with a more extensive client base. Apply for significant ventures and designed your proposition to grandstand your skill.

Organizing Chunks: Try not to misjudge the force of systems administration! Associate with other remote helpers, join online networks, and go to industry occasions. Verbal suggestions and references can be important wellsprings of new client open doors.

4. Conveying Worth and Building Trust:
Correspondence Champion: Proactive and predictable openness is of the utmost importance. Keep clients refreshed on progress, address concerns expeditiously, and effectively look for criticism to assemble trust and guarantee smooth coordinated efforts.

Expectation Expert: Try not to simply hang tight for guidelines! Expect your clients' requirements and proposition arrangements before they inquire. Propose upgrades and enhancing cycles to augment their worth.

Surpassing Assumptions: Convey flawless outcomes that reliably surpass client assumptions. Maintain elevated expectations of hard working attitude, comply with time constraints, and keep up with fastidious tender loving care. Your standing for dependability and greatness will draw in and hold clients.

5. Living Successfully Online:

Nonstop Learning Crusader: The menial helper scene is continually advancing. Remain refreshed on industry patterns, go to online courses, and seek after pertinent certificates to keep your range of abilities sharp and stay cutthroat.

Dynamo of Diversification: Think about offering a variety of services as your virtual assistant. Investigate related contributions like substance creation, accounting, or the Internet promoting to take care of more extensive client needs and make extra revenue sources.

Balance between fun and serious activities Wizard: Working remotely requires discipline. Lay out clear limits among work and individual life, set committed work hours, and focus on your prosperity to stay balanced and keep up with manageable achievement.

Keep in mind, the outcome in virtual help is an excursion, not an aim:

Embrace Input and Development: Effectively look for input from clients and partners. Examine your outcomes, recognize regions for development, and refine your method considering true information.

Construct a Strong Organization: Share your experiences with other virtual assistants and gain knowledge from them. A steady organization can be significant for inspiration, information sharing, and defeating difficulties.

Explore constantly: There are a lot of exciting options in the world of virtual help. Be available to new open doors, investigate various specialties, and remain inquisitive about developing patterns. Allow your enthusiasm and commitment to lead you to new heights of success!

I trust in your capability to turn into a flourishing remote helper and cut your own way to progress in this powerful field. By zeroing in on the areas that impact you, improving your abilities, conveying remarkable help, and embracing nonstop learning, you can make a satisfying and productive profession according to your own preferences.

These are only a couple of models, and the web-based world offers vast potential outcomes! Here are a few extra plans to ignite your pioneering soul:

Marketing via affiliates: You can earn commissions on sales you generate by promoting the products of other businesses.

Information passage and record: Convert recordings of audio or video into text for use by individuals and businesses.

Online instruction and tutoring: Share your insight and skill with understudies of any age through internet-based stages.

Website architecture and advancement: Fabricate dazzling sites and applications for clients out of luck.

Application improvement: Make portable applications that tackle issues and offer some incentive to clients.

Interpretation and translation: Span language boundaries and work with correspondence for organizations and people.

Content creation: Write compelling content for your website, social media posts, and articles.

digital book distributing: Reach a global audience by sharing your writing or expertise through self-published e-books.

Keep in mind, the way to progress in web-based locally established organizations is devotion, imagination, and versatility. Research your specialty, refine your contributions, and construct serious areas of strength for a presence. With the right method and a portion of Inhustle, the computerized world can be clam!

the following area, we'll investigate locally situated. Prepare to release your nearby pioneering soul and find adventures that flourish in the actual!

7. Remote helper

Chapter Three

13 Demonstrated Locally established Organisations (Offline).

Hoping to dump the drive and construct your own realm from the solace of home? For ambitious individuals seeking freedom and flexibility, the offline world provides a wealth of opportunities. The following are 13 moving locally situated business thoughts that flourish without depending only on the web:

1. Providing food and Individual Cook Administrations:

Offer catered meals for events, home-cooked meals for busy families, or customized meal plans for health-conscious individuals to test your culinary skills.

the flavorful universe of catering and individual cook administrations! A fabulous decision for energetic foodies needs to merge culinary inventiveness with the opportunity and adaptability of maintaining their own business. To dive further into this astonishing domain, what explicit parts of providing food and individual gourmet specialist administrations might you want to investigate? Here are a few choices:

1. Picking Your Specialty:
Catering Concentration: Will you have practical experience in occasion cooking, corporate snacks, personal

evening gatherings, or a particular food? Characterizing your specialty helps focus on your showcasing and draw in the right customers.

Individual Culinary specialist Approach: Do you imagine offering week by week feast plans, one-off unique event dinners, cooking classes, or dietary-explicit choices? Reduce your focus to meet a particular need or preference.

2. Building Your Culinary Armory:

Culinary Mastery: Get experience working in a restaurant kitchen, professional training, or culinary courses to improve your cooking skills. Dominating various foods and dietary prerequisites will expand your allure.

Gear and Supplies: Put resources into top-notch kitchen instruments, food capacity compartments, and show gear to guarantee proficient execution and effective work.

Menu planning and recipe creation: Design appealing menus that showcase your culinary style and meet the preferences of your customers, while also catering to a variety of dietary requirements and creating signature dishes.

3. Exploring the Business Side:
Permitting and Allows: Research and gain vital allows and licenses for food dealing with and business activities in your area.
Protection Inclusion: Secure responsibility protection to shield your business from unanticipated episodes.
Setting Cutthroat Rates: Calculate food costs, planning time, above costs, and wanted net revenue to lie out aggressive and manageable evaluating structures.

4. Showcasing and Drawing in Clients:
Building a Portfolio: Feature your culinary abilities through photographs, client tributes, and online presence.

Make a site or web-based entertainment profiles to share your menus and administrations.

Systems administration and Nearby Associations: Assemble associations with occasion organizers, party scenes, nearby organizations, and likely clients to get the message out about your administrations.

Offering Motivating forces and bundles: Plan extraordinary cooking bundles, offer preliminary feast designs, or give limits to references to draw in new clients and stand apart from the opposition.

5. Conveying Remarkable help:
Stunning Food and Show: Center on heavenly flavors, great fixings, and imaginative show to intrigue your clients and surpass their assumptions.
Incredible skill and Correspondence: Be able to adapt to the needs and requests of your customers while maintaining a

professional demeanor and clear communication with them.

Developing Loyalty and Trust: Offer customized help, recall client inclinations, and exceed everyone's expectations to construct solid connections and secure recurrent business.

Keep in mind, the outcome in providing food and individual culinary specialist administrations takes time and commitment:

Refine Your Contributions: Ceaselessly try different things with new recipes, update your menus, and adjust your administrations in view of client criticism to remain new and pertinent.

Put resources into Proficient Turn of events: Go to culinary studios, food styling courses, or business workshops to improve your abilities and keep up to date with industry patterns.

Establish a Supportive Circle: interface with different caterers, individual culinary experts, and food industry experts to share information, team up on projects, and gain from one another's encounters.

I'm here to be your confided in culinary friend on this astonishing excursion! Pose a particular inquiry about menu arranging, valuing techniques, promoting your administrations, or exploring the coordinated operations of catering an occasion. Together, we should transform your culinary enthusiasm into a flourishing providing food or individual gourmet specialist business!

Keep in mind, the kitchen is your material, and the conceivable outcomes are huge! Bon appétit!

2. Locally established Bread shop or Candy store:

Prepare scrumptious treats and heated merchandise from your own kitchen, selling them at nearby business sectors, ranchers' business sectors, or running a conveyance administration for sweet-toothed clients.

Ok, the sweet universe of locally situated pastry shops and candy parlors! It's a brilliant decision for enthusiastic dough punchers with a talent for transforming fixings into eatable magnum opuses. What specific aspects of starting your own home-based bakery or confectionery would you like to investigate in order to delve deeper into this enticing field?

Here are a few choices:

1. Characterizing Your Sweet Specialty:
Bread kitchen Concentration: Will you work in breads, baked goods, cakes,

treats, or a particular food? Recognizing your specialty helps focus on your market and draw on the right customer base.

Ice cream parlor Pleasures: Will you center on chocolates, macaroons, truffles, distinctive pastries, or custom sugar workmanship? You stand out from the competition by defining your distinctive offerings.

2. Learning the Art of Baking:
Culinary Mastery: Level up your baking abilities through proficient preparation, recipe trial and error, and practice to guarantee predictable quality and tasty outcomes.

Kitchen Hardware and Supplies: For effective and professional work, make an investment in high-quality baking tools, ovens, mixers, storage containers, and presentation equipment.

Recipe Improvement and Menu Arranging: Make signature prepared products, take special care of dietary requirements, and configuration engaging menus that grandstand your imaginative pizazz and take special care of client inclinations.

3. Exploring the Business Side:
Neighborhood Guidelines and Grants: Research and get important allows and licenses for locally situated food creation in your area.
Protection Inclusion: Secure responsibility protection to safeguard your business from unexpected occurrences.
Setting Serious Costs: Figure fixing costs, baking time, above costs, and wanted overall revenue to lie out reasonably evaluating structures.

4. Improving the Promoting Blend:
Marking and Online Presence: Foster an outwardly engaging logo, site, and virtual entertainment profiles to grandstand your contributions and interface with clients.

Neighborhood Associations and Systems administration: Fabricate associations with bistros, cafes, ranchers' business sectors, and occasion coordinators to grow your span and sell your prepared products.

Limited time Techniques and Offers: Offer preliminary boxes, make tempting treat bundles, run extraordinary advancements, and influence positive audits and tributes to draw in new clients.

5. Conveying Sweet help and Quality:

Wonderful Flavors and Show: Center on new fixings, heavenly recipes, and innovative show to dazzle your clients and surpass their assumptions.

Amazing skill and correspondence: Keep an expert disposition, discuss plainly with clients, and be versatile to oblige their necessities and solicitations.

Building Trust and Dedication: Give reliably top notch items, recall client inclinations, and go above and beyond to assemble solid connections and secure recurrent business.

Keep in mind, the outcome in a locally situated pastry kitchen or ice cream parlor takes time and devotion:

Persistent Improvement: Explore different avenues regarding new recipes, update your menus, and adjust to showcase patterns to keep your contributions new and energizing.

Proficient Turn of events: Go to baking studios, food styling courses, and business classes to upgrade your abilities and keep up to date with industry advancements.

Building a Strong Organization: Interface with other home bread cooks, confectioners, and food industry experts to share information, team up on projects, and gain from one another's encounters.

I'm here to be your confided in baking sidekick on this sweet excursion! Pose a particular inquiry about recipe improvement, valuing systems, showcasing your pastry kitchen, or exploring the coordinated factors of locally situated creation. Together, we should transform your baking enthusiasm into a flourishing locally situated pastry kitchen or dessert shop that improves everybody's day!

Keep in mind, your imagination is the key to fixing! In this way, dust off your cover, preheat your broiler, and how about we prepare your fantasies for the real world!

3. Specialty and craftworker Merchandise Creation:

Channel your imagination by creating hand tailored gems, extras, home stylistic layout things, or other special items to sell locally at make fairs, shops, or through direct web-based channels.

The universe of specialties and craftworker merchandise is a gold mine of imagination, expertise, and vast conceivable outcomes! Whether you're a carefully prepared potter, a fastidious knitter, or a carpentry wizard, changing your enthusiasm into a locally established business can unimaginably satisfy. To dig further into this thrilling domain, we should investigate explicit parts of beginning your own specialty and craftworker merchandise creation:

1. Characterizing Your Art Specialty:
Medium and Method: Will you work in ceramics, gems, material specialties, carpentry, or a novel mix? Zeroing in on

a particular medium refines your skill and draws in designated clients.

Item Concentration: Will you make useful things like mugs and bowls, beautifying pieces like models and compositions, or wearable craftsmanship like gems and embellishments? Recognizing your item range directs your plan and creation process.

2. Leveling up Your Art Abilities:

Persistent Learning: Take studios, online courses, or look for mentorship from experienced craftworker to refine your current abilities and investigate new procedures.

Quality and Consistency: Execute quality control gauges and take a stab at predictable outcomes in your craftwork to construct a standing for dependable greatness.

Innovation and Experimentation: try different things with new materials, plans, and methods to keep your manifestations new and remarkable.

3. Building Your Creation Munititions stockpile:

Fundamental Apparatuses and Hardware: Put resources into top-notch instruments and gear well defined for your picked specialty to guarantee effective and proficient creation.

Material getting: Research solid provides for quality unrefined substances, watching out for moral getting and maintainability rehearses.

Work area Improvement: Set up a committee work area in your home that cultivates imagination, association, and an effective creation stream.

4. Exploring the Business Side:

Lawful and Administrative System: Secure any vital licenses or allow for locally situated creation and art deals in your area.

Management of finances: Track your costs, computer creation expenses, and set serious costs with a solid net revenue.

Protection Inclusion: If you want to safeguard your company from unforeseen events, think about purchasing liability insurance.

5. Exhibiting Your Craftsmanship:
Marking and Online Presence: Foster a dazzling brand character, site, and virtual entertainment profiles that grandstand your exceptional style and item contributions.

Selling Stages: Investigate different deals channels like web-based commercial centers, Etsy shops, make fairs, neighborhood showcases, and direct deals to clients.

Promoting and Narrating: Share the story behind your art, associate with expected clients on a profound level, and use viable showcasing techniques to stand out.

6. Conveying Quality and Building Trust:

Dazzling Workmanship and Scrupulousness: To ensure customer satisfaction, focus on exceptional quality, finishing touches, and meticulous presentation.

Client support Greatness: Answer instantly to requests, offer customized administration, and address any worries with impressive skill and care.

Building a local area: To build strong relationships and a loyal clientele, interact with customers, gather feedback, and actively take part in the craft community.

Keep in mind, progress in art and craftworker merchandise creation takes time and devotion:

Continual Development: To stay ahead of the curve, you should never stop learning new things, honing your skills, and adjusting to market trends.

Systems administration and Cooperation: Explore collaboration opportunities, attend industry events, and connect with other craftspeople to expand your reach and gain knowledge from one another.

Building Strength and Enthusiasm: Embrace the difficulties of maintaining a locally situated business, remain consistent with your innovative vision, and let your enthusiasm guide you through snags.

I'm here to help you along on this thrilling journey! You are welcome to ask any specific inquiries regarding the selection of your craft niche, pricing strategies, product marketing, or navigating your home-based craft business's production and logistics. Together, we should move your inventive flash toward a flourishing specialty and craftworker merchandise creation adventure that gives pleasure to both you and your clients!

Keep in mind that you can turn your passion into a lucrative and fulfilling craft business with hard work, skill, and a dash of creative magic. Along these lines, put on your innovative cap, snatch your apparatuses, and we should leave on this imaginative experience together!

4. Services for Childcare and Babysitting:

Offer protected and solid childcare in your own home or give minding to families in your area, fabricating a standing as a confided in gatekeeper for priceless little ones.

The field of child care and babysitting provides a satisfying opportunity to care for young children and establish dependable relationships with families. Whether you're a carefully prepared childcare proficient or simply beginning, I'm here to assist you with exploring the way to outcome in this satisfying field.

To begin, we should investigate a few explicit parts of offering childcare and minding from your home:

1. Characterizing Your Extent of Administrations:

Age Group: Will you concentrate on infants, toddlers, and preschoolers, or will you cover a wider age range?

Administrations Advertised: Will you provide activities, educational play, help with homework, or meal preparation besides basic care?

Booking Choices: Will you offer full-time care, part-time timetables, end of the week gigs, or infrequent looking after children?

2. Building Your Mastery and Capabilities:

Training and certification: Consider seeking after childcare confirmations, CPR preparing, and emergency treatment preparing to exhibit your commitment and information.

References and Experience: Feature any applicable experience working with kids, for example, chipping in, nannying, or minding.

Individual Characteristics: Underline your understanding, warmth, inventiveness, and capacity to interface with offspring of various ages and characters.

3. Laying out a Safe and Supporting Climate:

Home Security: Guarantee your house is childproofed, with secure outlets, age-proper toys, and clear wellbeing conventions.

Play Region and Exercises: Make an assigned play region loaded with drawing in toys, books, and exercises that invigorate learning and improvement.

Crisis Readiness: Foster a reasonable arrangement for taking care of crises, including fire drills, medical aid techniques, and contact data for guardians.

4. Getting Customers and Establishing Trust:

Informal Promoting: Influence positive verbal exchange proposals from companions, family, and past clients.

Online Presence: Make an expert site or profile on childcare stages to grandstand your administrations and experience.

Systems administration and local area associations: Increase your visibility and the number of potential customers you can attract by establishing connections with families, schools, and community centers in the area.

5. Conveying Remarkable Consideration and Building Connections:

Individualized Focus: Get to know every youngster's extraordinary necessities and inclinations to give customized care and exercises.

Correspondence and straightforwardness: Keep up with open correspondence with guardians, update them on their kid's advancement, and address any worries quickly.

Positive and Drawing in Climate: Cultivate a tomfoolery, safe, and good climate where kids feel great and can learn and develop.

Keep in mind, progress in childcare and watching on devotion, obligation, and veritable love for youngsters:

Ceaseless Learning: Keep up with the latest developments in educational methods, safety guidelines, and best practices for child development.

Incredible skill and Unwavering quality: Maintain exclusive requirements of amazing skill, keep up with reliability, and exhibit obligation to your clients.

Assembling Long haul Connections: attempt to earn the trust and positive relationships of families by going above and beyond to establish a stable and nurturing care environment for their children.

Regardless of your involvement, with the right method and an energy for childcare, you can construct a flourishing locally established business and have a beneficial outcome to the existences of kids and families.

Keep in mind, each kid merits a sustaining and strong climate, and you can assume an imperative part in giving that through your childcare and watching. Go forward and spread your adoration and information, each little experience!

5. Pet sitting and Canine strolling:

Creature darlings can transform their energy into a flourishing business by offering pet sitting administrations, canine strolling, or even pet instructional courses, dealing with shaggy companions while their proprietors are away.

Absolutely! The universe of pet consideration offers an abundance of chances for creature darlings to fabricate satisfying and productive locally established organizations. Whether you're a canine whisperer, a feline friend, or a reptile enthusiast, you can transform your enthusiasm into a flourishing endeavor by offering types of help like:

1. Pet Sitting:

In-home pet sitting: Give friendship, taking care of, recess, and essential consideration for creatures in their own homes while proprietors are away.

Overnight lodging: Offer sleepovers at your home for pets who lean toward a natural climate or require extraordinary consideration.

Drop-in visits: Make many visits over the course of the day for taking care of, potty breaks, and recess to guarantee shaggy companions stay blissful and animated.

2. Canine Strolling and Canine Running:
Group or one-on-one walks: Take care of explicit requirements and inclinations, offering solo strolls for apprehensive little guys or fiery gathering strolls for outgoing people.

Off-chain experiences: Give controlled, safe, and fun investigations in closed in regions for athletic canines who flourish with opportunity.

Extraordinary necessities contemplations: Oblige senior canines, young doggies, or canines with explicit restrictions to guarantee charming and agreeable strolls.

3. Training a Pet:

Basic training in obedience: For improved communication and a well-behaved pet, teach basic commands like sit, stay, heel, and come.

Potty preparation and changing outwardly: Address undesirable ways of behaving like yapping, biting, or going through uplifting feedback and delicate direction.

Individualized training plans: Configuration is customized preparing plans to address explicit requirements and difficulties, from rope reactivity to housebreaking obstacles.

4. Extra Administrations:

Pet transportation: Provide secure and dependable transportation for grooming sessions, vet visits, and other outings.

Removal of pet waste: Provide pet owners who lack the time or ability to deal with messy tasks with pet waste cleanup services.

Intelligent pet games and exercises: Draw in with pets through puzzle games, find the stowaway, or tomfoolery bring meetings for mental excitement and improvement.

Building an Effective Pet Consideration Business:

Nearby licenses and allows: Research and get any essential allows or licenses expected for working a pet consideration business in your space.

Protection inclusion: Secure responsibility protection to shield your business from unanticipated occurrences.

Security and experience: Accentuate your obligation to pet security, creature conduct information, and applicable involvement with working with various kinds of creatures.

Promoting and organizing: Construct associations with pet people through nearby postings, online stages, web-based entertainment, and references from fulfilled clients.

Uncommon help and devotion: Focus on creature government help, give cherishing and mindful consideration, and endeavor to surpass client assumptions to fabricate solid long haul connections.

Keep in mind, progress in pet consideration requires certifiable love for creatures, a pledge to their prosperity, and a devotion to giving dependable and great administrations. You can turn your animal-loving nature into a thriving home-based business that meets the needs of pets and brings joy to their owners with passion, knowledge, and strategic planning.

Pose a particular inquiry you have about beginning your pet consideration business! Whether it's picking your specialty, valuing your administrations, showcasing your mastery, or exploring the coordinated operations of really focusing on different creatures, I'm here to be your steady aide and assist you with making a fruitful and satisfying endeavor in the compensating universe of pet consideration.

How about we sway a few tails and make those shaggy companions murmur with joy together!

6. Home Improvement and Jack of all trades Administrations:

Assuming you're gifted in fixes, support, and limited scope Do-It-Yourself projects, you can take special care of your neighbourhood local area by offering jack of all trades administrations, repairing homes, and handling those bothersome daily agendas for occupied property holders.

The universe of home improvement and jack of all trades administrations coaxes every one of those with a tool stash loaded with abilities and an enthusiasm for fixing things! On the off chance that you're hoping to construct a locally established business in this domain, we should dig into a few vital viewpoints to consider:

1. Characterizing Your Specialty:

General Jack of all trades: Offer an expansive scope of administrations like minor pipes fixes, carpentry work, painting, and installation establishments.

Particular Skills: Center on specialty regions like electrical work, machine fix, tiling, or drywall establishment to draw in unambiguous customer base.

Audience in Mind: Take care of property holders, landowners, business spaces, or explicit socioeconomics like senior residents requiring availability adjustments.

2. Building Your Tool compartment and Aptitude:

Fundamental Devices and Gear: Put resources into excellent apparatuses and security gear well defined for the administrations you offer.

Constant Learning: Go to studios, online courses, or shadow experienced experts to level up your abilities and remain refreshed on industry patterns.

Wellbeing and Permitting: Acquire the licenses, permits, and insurance to operate safely and legally, as well as comprehend local regulations.

3. Creating Your Workplace and Home Base:

Devoted Workspace: Upgrade a carport, shed, or storm cellar into an exceptional work area for project planning and stockpiling.

Portable Tasks: For smooth travel and effective on-site service delivery, invest in a dependable vehicle and organize tools.

Stock Administration: Keep a supplied stock of usually used parts and materials to keep away from delays and guarantee project finishing.

4. Drawing in Clients and Building Trust:

Verbal Showcasing: Urge past clients to get the news out about your solid administrations and quality work.

Online Presence: Make an expert site or profiles on nearby help stages to exhibit your abilities and skill.

Local Connections: For referral opportunities, build relationships with real estate agents, property managers, and other community contacts.

5. Conveying First class Administration and Building Worth:

Free Gauges and Clear Correspondence: Give straightforward valuing gauges and keep up with open correspondence with clients throughout the undertaking.

Impressive skill and unwavering quality: Show up on time, regard client property, and guarantee top notch workmanship in each errand.

Exceeding everyone's expectations: To exceed expectations, provide additional services like furniture assembly, minor landscaping, or home improvement advice.

Keep in mind that continual improvement and dedication are necessary for success in handyman services and home improvement.

Remaining Refreshed: Go to expos, industry occasions, and item shows to find out about new apparatuses, materials, and procedures.

Client Connections and Subsequent meet-ups: Give support suggestions, crisis fix benefits, and follow-up calls to construct long haul trust and rehash business.

Building a Positive Standing: Effectively look for client criticism, address concerns speedily, and take a stab at reliably certain encounters to harden your standing as a solid and dependable jack of all trades.

I'm here to be your steady sidekick on this excursion! Ask questions you might have about pricing your services, marketing your business, complying with legal requirements, or locating resources that can help you improve your skills and knowledge. Together, we should transform your jack of all trades soul into a flourishing locally established business that tackles issues, enhances homes, and leaves clients happy with each tap, switch, and nail pounded in!

Keep in mind, each fix, each redesign, each improvement adds to making better living spaces and more joyful networks. In this way, get your tool kit, release your inward McGyver, and how about we construct something fantastic together!

7. Individual Preparation and Wellness Training:

Share your energy for wellness by offering customized instructional courses in your own home exercise center, park, or outside, assisting clients with accomplishing their wellness objectives and lift their prosperity.

Ok, the universe of individual preparation and wellness instructing! It's a domain where energy for wellness meets the delight of engaging others to accomplish their wellbeing and health objectives. On the off chance that you're longing to build a flourishing locally established business in this thrilling field, we should investigate a few critical perspectives to consider:

1. Choosing Your Method and Niche:

Preparing Style: Will you center on extreme focus exercises, customized schedules, practical preparation, or a particular wellness method like yoga or Pilates?

Ideal interest group: Will you take care of general wellness lovers, competitors, weight reduction objectives, explicit populaces like seniors or pre-natal clients?

Area Inclinations: Offer in-home instructional courses, outside exercises, virtual training, or a blend, considering your client base and assets.

2. Building Your Ability and Capabilities:

Training and certification: Through workshops and courses, you can get certified in personal training that is recognized by the industry and keep up with industry trends.

Wellness information and experience: Clients are more likely to trust you if you can show solid fitness knowledge, practical skills, and relevant experience.

Emergency treatment and CPR accreditation: Be ready to deal with crises and guarantee client security during instructional courses.

3. Establishing a Steady Preparation Climate:

Protected and Prepared Space: Whether inside or outside, guarantee your preparation space is protected, exceptional, and helpful for successful exercises.

Persuasive air: Establish a positive and empowering climate that encourages client commitment and objective accomplishment.

Individualized plans and modifications: Foster individualized preparing plans and adjust schedules in view of every client's wellness level, objectives, and impediments.

4. Drawing in Clients and Building an Organization:

Informal exchange promoting: Your best advocates are content customers. Support references and influence positive tributes to draw in new clients.

Online presence: Foster an expert site and online entertainment profiles displaying your mastery, preparing style, and client examples of overcoming adversity.

Network with neighborhood exercise centers, wellbeing focuses, and health experts: Assemble connections and potential reference valuable open doors inside the wellness local area.

5. Conveying Outstanding help and Motivating Outcomes:

Client-centered approach: Focus on your clients' objectives, needs, and solace level to make a customized and compensating preparing experience.

Responsibility and inspiration: Energize consistency, track progress, and offer continuous help to keep clients roused and on target.

Positive correspondence and input: Keep up with open correspondence, effectively pay attention to clients' interests, and give helpful input to guarantee ideal outcomes.

Keep in mind, the outcome in private preparation and wellness training takes commitment and ceaseless improvement.

Put money into your fitness: Remain effectively took part in your own wellness process to set a positive model and keep up with your own preparation information sharp.

Plan adjustments and client progress tracking: Consistently evaluate client progress, change preparing schedules depending on the situation, and praise each achievement accomplished together.

Support a positive local area: Fabricate a local area around your clients through wellness challenges, bunch meetings, or online care groups to cultivate inspiration and association.

I'm here to be your confided in consultant and team promoter on this thrilling excursion! Ask questions you may have about starting a home-based personal training business, pricing your services, creating efficient training programs, or navigating the complexities of running one. Together, we should transform your energy for wellness into a flourishing endeavor that engages people to arrive at their wellbeing and health objectives and become their best selves!

Keep in mind that your dedication and the inspiring impact you have on the lives of your clients are demonstrated by every drop of sweat, every broken record, and every step closer to achieving a goal. Thus, ribbon up your shoes, get your water jug, and we should leave on this excursion of changing bodies and building a local area of enabled people, each exercise!

8. Music Illustrations and Mentoring:

On the off chance that you have melodic mastery or information on a specific subject, offer confidential examples from your home, taking care of understudies looking for direction in music, dialects, scholastics, or explicit abilities.

Ok, the charming universe of music illustrations and mentoring! It's where your energy for music entwines with the delight of directing others in their melodic excursion. Whether you're a carefully prepared virtuoso or a committed music sweetheart, fabricating a flourishing locally established business in this field can staggeringly compensate. How about we investigate a few critical viewpoints to consider:

1. Characterizing Your Melodic Specialty:

Instruments: Will you have practical experience in piano, guitar, drums, vocals, or a more extensive scope of instruments?

Kinds and Styles: Do you succeed in old style, jazz, rock, pop, or a particular melodic type?

Interest group: Will you center on fledglings, middle students, yearning experts, or explicit age bunches like kids or seniors?

2. Building Your Melodic Stockpile and Skill:

Formal Music Preparing: Show your capability through music degrees, recognitions, or confirmation programs pertinent to your picked instrument and instructing style.

Execution Experience: Sharing your own melodic excursion through exhibitions can move and spur your understudies.

Continuous Education: Go to studios, masterclasses, and proficient advancement exercises to remain refreshed on new showing strategies and music patterns.

3. Stimulating the Learning Environment
Dedicated Space for Music: Install high-quality instruments, soundproofing, and comfortable seating in your home's practice room.

Adaptable Illustration Configurations: Offer individual illustrations, bunch meetings, online music educational cost, or mixed learning choices to take care of assorted learning inclinations.

Drawing in Educating Materials: To keep students interested and motivated, make use of creative teaching strategies, individualized exercises, interactive tools, and entertaining activities.

4. Drawing in Understudies and Building an Organization:

Informal Advertising: Urge fulfilled understudies to get the news out about your uncommon showing abilities and positive acquiring climate.

Online Presence: Make an expert site and virtual entertainment profiles exhibiting your capabilities, music mastery, and understudy tributes.

Neighborhood Associations: Collaborate with music schools, instrument stores, public venues, or school music projects to grow your compass and draw in likely understudies.

5. Providing Good Instruction and Promoting Development:

Customized Learning: Tailor your illustrations to every understudy's singular necessities, learning speed, and melodic objectives.

Uplifting feedback and Support: Give useful criticism, praise accomplishments, and cultivate a steady climate that empowers investigation and development.

Execution Amazing open doors: Create recitals, workshops, or ensemble activities for students to gain experience performing and boost confidence.

Keep in mind, progress in music illustrations and mentoring requires continuous devotion and improvement:

Keep Motivated: Learn constantly, playing, and investigating your own melodic interests to fuel your energy and move your understudies.

Embrace Innovation: Use advanced devices, music applications, and online assets to upgrade your examples and take care of current learning styles.

Support a Local area: Through workshops, jam sessions, or online music forums, foster a supportive community among your students to foster collaboration and passion.

Keep in mind, each note played, each harmony dominated, each tune learned is a demonstration of your devotion and the extraordinary force of music. Thus, tune your instruments, snatch your printed music, and we should leave on this delightful excursion of imparting your melodic information and enthusiasm to the world, each understudy in turn!

9. Occasion Arranging and Party Plan:

From your home office, you can help clients create memorable celebrations by planning and designing events like weddings, birthday parties, and corporate gatherings. This will let you show off your organizational skills and creative flair.

The universe of occasion arranging and party configuration is a stunning kaleidoscope of innovativeness, association, and the delight of making remarkable encounters! Whether you're a speaker or a mysterious Pinterest wizard, fabricating a flourishing locally situated business in this domain can be as satisfying as it is merry. We should investigate a few vital viewpoints to make way for your prosperity:

1. Characterizing Your Occasion Specialty:

Specialties: Will you center around weddings, corporate occasions, confidential gatherings, themed get-togethers, or a particular sort like celebrations or Jewish rights of passage?

Client Concentration: Do you flourish with top of the line extravagance occasions, cozy parties, or thrifty festivals?

Area Inclinations: Offer in-home discussions, setting obtaining, virtual preparation, or a blend in view of your assets and client needs.

2. Becoming amazing at Party Plan:

Pattern Following and Motivation: Keep up to date with occasion configuration patterns, investigate different party subjects, and develop an interesting complex vision.

Negotiation and expertise in the venue: Foster information on nearby scenes, grasp contracts, and explore exchanges for ideal areas and spending plan contemplations.

Merchant and Asset Organization: Assemble associations with food providers, decorators, flower vendors, picture takers, and other occasion experts to offer complete administrations.

3. Coordinating an Impeccable Occasion:

Planned operations and Association: For a successful event, master the timelines, budgets, vendor coordination, seating plans, and contingency plans.

Project The executives and Correspondence: Keep up with clear correspondence with clients, sellers, and scene staff to guarantee everybody is in total agreement.

Resolving issues and being flexible: Embrace the unforeseen, think and react quickly, and promptly adjust to difficulties or last-minute changes.

4. Promoting Your Party Magic:

Portfolio and Contextual analyses: Exhibit your previous occasion manifestations through dazzling photographs, tributes, and point by point contextual analyses.

Computerized Presence: Fabricate an expert site and dynamic virtual entertainment profiles that feature your plan vision, administrations, and client fulfillment.

Systems administration and Joint effort: Associate with wedding organizers, setting directors, party supply stores, and other occasion experts for likely references and organizations.

5. Conveying Extraordinary Encounters and Building Recollections:

Customized Touch and Imaginative Energy: Inject every occasion with your special plan contact, consolidating the client's vision and making a customized environment.

Surpassing Assumptions and Scrupulousness: Endeavor to reliably exceed all expectations, guaranteeing each component adds to an immaculate and important experience.

Building Client Connections and Trust: Focus on client correspondence, effectively pay attention to their requirements, and fabricate long haul connections for rehash business and references.

Keep in mind, outcome in occasion arranging and party configuration requires steady development and a bold soul:

Nonstop Learning: Go to studios, gatherings, and industry occasions to remain refreshed on patterns, network with experts, and level up your abilities.

Embrace Innovation: Event planning software, design tools, and online resources can be used to improve efficiency and incorporate novel elements into your events.

Local area Building: Cultivate associations with clients, merchants, and individual occasion experts to make a steady organization and offer thoughts.

Keep in mind, each fastidiously arranged detail, each act of kindness, each snapshot of chuckling and happiness shared is a demonstration of your abilities and the enchanted you bring to the universe of occasions. Thus, get your party cap, release your inventiveness, and we should kick this festival off!

10. Locally situated Photography Administrations:

Set out to really utilise your focal point by offering picture photography, family photograph meetings, item photography for neighbourhood organisations, or even occasion photography, catching unique minutes from the solace of your own studio.

The universe of locally situated photography offers you the wonderful chance to catch life's minutes, recount stories from your perspective, and fabricate a flourishing business right from your own space. Let's take a look at the most important aspects of turning your photographic vision into a profitable home-based business, whether you're an experienced shutterbug or an enthusiastic amateur:

1. Characterizing Your Specialty and Specializations:

Representation Photography: Center around family pictures, infant photography, proficient headshots, or boudoir meetings.

Occasion Photography: Catch weddings, birthday celebrations, graduations, corporate occasions, or get-togethers.

Item Photography: Assist organizations feature their items with effective symbolism for the end goal of showcasing.

Land Photography: Photograph homes in a stunning way to help real estate agents attract buyers.

2. Building Your Photography Munititions stockpile and Abilities:

Equipment and a Camera of High Quality: For professional results, invest in a suitable camera, lenses, lighting setups, and editing software.

Specialized Mastery and Organization Abilities: Create compelling images by mastering camera settings, lighting techniques, and composition principles.

Prowess in Post-Processing and Editing: Learn proficient altering methods to upgrade your photographs and add your creative touch.

3. Making an Inviting and Effective Home Studio (Discretionary):

Devoted Photography Space: Upgrade a room in your home with legitimate lighting, sceneries, props, and agreeable client regions.

Versatile Studio Arrangement: Pack your gear for area shoots and be ready to adjust to assorted conditions.

Association and Work process: use effective workflows for image capture, editing, and client communication to streamline your procedure.

4. Drawing in Clients and Building an Organization:

Informal Advertising: Encourage happy customers to tell others about your talent and outstanding service.

Online Presence: Make an expert site and online entertainment profiles displaying your portfolio, abilities, and client tributes.

Local Connections: Interface with photographic artists, occasion organizers, organizations, and local area associations for likely references and coordinated efforts.

5. Conveying Quality Photography and Building Solid Connections:

Pre-Shoot Meetings: To guarantee successful outcomes, you must comprehend client expectations, discuss preferences, and collaborate on the planning of shoots.

Reliability and Professionalism: Show up on time, be ready, and impart really throughout the whole cycle.

Innovative Narrating and Imaginative Vision: Catch valid minutes, infuse your extraordinary style, and convey pictures that resound with your clients.

Keep in mind, the outcome in locally situated photography depends on steady development and devotion:

Keep Learning and Testing: Go to studios, online courses, and photography occasions to refine your abilities and investigate new procedures.

Put resources into Your Business: Think about proficient marking, showcasing systems, and systems administration valuable chances to grow your compass and draw in new clients.

Center on Client Fulfillment: Establishing positive relationships with your customers, actively meeting their requirements, and constantly striving to meet or exceed they expect priorities.

I'm here to be your strong aide and sidekick on this innovative excursion! Pose a particular inquiry you have about picking your specialty, setting up your home studio, estimating your administrations, showcasing your photography business, or exploring the specialized parts of catching dazzling pictures. Together, we should transform your enthusiasm for photography into a flourishing locally situated adventure that catches life's valuable minutes and passes on your clients with enduring recollections to esteem.

Keep in mind, each snap of the shade, each glimmer of motivation, each picture recounting a story is a demonstration of your creative vision and the delight you bring from your perspective. Thus, snatch your camera, embrace your inventiveness, and we should set out on this wonderful excursion of changing light into immortal photos, each picture!

11. Sewing and Changes Administration.

Offer clothing alterations, repairs, or even custom-made garments to customers who value quality craftsmanship and personalized clothing solutions and put your needle and thread skills to use.

Releasing Your Inward Fasten Wizard: Sending off a Locally situated Sewing and Modifications Administration

If you're enthusiastic about changing textures and making pieces of clothing fit like a fantasy, a locally situated sewing and modifications business can be a fulfilling and imaginative endeavor. We should fasten an arrangement for progress:

1. Characterizing Your Art and Specialty:

Various Modifications: Provide alterations, hemming, repairs, and resizing for a wide range of garments.

Specific Concentration: Consider marriage modifications, custom fitting, outfit plan, or working with explicit textures like calfskin or sensitive materials.

Innovative Administrations: Investigate custom sewing projects, clothing upcycling, or home stylistic theme things to grow your contributions.

2. Preparing Your Sewing Asylum:

Fundamental Devices: Put resources into a dependable sewing machine, serger, pressing board, dress structures, estimating devices, and various strings, needles, and scissors.

Coordinated Work area: Set up a committed sewing region in your home with adequate capacity for textures, devices, and ventures.

Proficient Completion: Guarantee is a spotless and sufficiently bright space to give an agreeable climate to clients.

3. Dominating Your Abilities and Strategies:

Central Sewing Strategies: Improve your skills at reading patterns, cutting, sewing, finishing seams, and making adjustments to fit.

Different Texture Information: Comprehend the properties and care necessities of various textures to guarantee quality outcomes.

Remain Refreshed: Go to studios, online courses, or join sewing networks to learn new methods and patterns.

4. Building Relationships and Attracting Customers

Verbal exchange Sorcery: Encourage happy customers to tell others about your expertise and attention to detail.

Online Presence: Create a professional website or social media profile that highlights your experience, products, and reviews from satisfied customers.

Nearby Organizations: Associate with dress stores, cleaners, wedding shops, or local area theater bunches for references.

5. Conveying Remarkable Help and Sewing Bliss:

Meeting and Correspondence: Comprehend client needs, talk about assumptions, and give clear timetables and valuing gauges.

Exact Estimations and fittings: Guarantee precision and scrupulousness for amazing fit and complimenting results.

Prompt and professional service: Regard cutoff times and convey articles of clothing in perfect condition, prepared to wear.

Keep in mind, the outcome in sewing and changes requires energy, tolerance, and a sharp eye for detail:

Consistent Learning: Explore constantly new methods, textures, and configuration patterns to grow your collection.

Business Basics: Handle funds, showcasing, and client correspondence really to guarantee a workable endeavor.

Client Fulfillment: Focus on superb client support, assemble confiding in connections, and effectively address any worries to empower rehash business and references.

I'm here to be your strong string guide and imaginative compatriot! Pose any inquiries you have about picking your specialty, estimating your administrations, getting materials, promoting your business, or dominating explicit sewing strategies. Together, we should transform your enthusiasm for sewing into a flourishing locally situated business that retouches, changes, and makes wonderfully fitting pieces of clothing, each join!

12. Locally situated Magnificence Administrations:

Offer salon-quality administrations like hair styles, nail treatments, facials, or back rubs right from your home, furnishing clients with a helpful and spoiling escape from the buzzing about.

The universe of locally established magnificence administrations entices every one of those with an adoration for spoiling, a talent for improving normal excellence, and a craving to construct a flourishing business right from their own space. Whether you're a cosmetics maestro, a skincare intellectual, or a nail workmanship ninja, we should dive into the vital parts of transforming your magnificence vision into an effective locally situated adventure:

1. Characterizing Your Specialty and Specializations:

Cosmetics Imaginativeness: Center on unique event cosmetics, marriage glitz, regular cosmetics instructional exercises, or customized cosmetics illustrations.

Skincare and facials: Offer facials custom fitted to various skin types, waxing, stringing, or temple molding administrations.

Nail Creativity: Exhibit your abilities in nail trims, pedicures, many-sided nail workmanship plans, or gel/acrylic augmentations.

Removal of hair: Give waxing, sugaring, or stringing administrations for different body regions.

Knead Treatment: Offer loosening up kneads, specific strategies like profound tissue or hot stone, or portable seat rub administrations.

2. Developing Your Beauty Tools and Techniques:

Excellent Items and Gear: Put resources into proficient grade cosmetics brushes, skincare devices, top-notch nail cleans, or back rub carries out relying upon your picked administration.

Control Information and Strategies: Ace your picked region, whether it's comprehension appearances, the most recent cosmetics patterns, perplexing nail craftsmanship strategies, or viable back rub techniques.

Cleanliness and Disinfection: Focus on a perfect and disinfected working climate, following severe cleanliness conventions and keeping up with clean devices.

3. Making an Unwinding and Inviting Home Salon (Discretionary):

Specialized Beauty Room: A relaxing atmosphere, comfortable seating, adequate lighting, storage for products and equipment, and optimization of a room in your home are all important.

Versatile Magnificence Arrangement: Pack your basis for on location arrangements and guarantee effective arrangement/breakdown processes.

Client Solace and Comfort: Offer refreshments, music, or different conveniences to improve the client experience.

4. Building a Clientele and a Network:
Informal Advertising: Encourage happy customers to tell others about your expertise and exceptional service.

Online Presence: Make an expert site or online entertainment profiles exhibiting your skill, portfolio, and client tributes.

Nearby Systems administration: Interface with salons, spas, occasion organizers, or wellness places for references and joint efforts.

Designated Offers and Advancements: Think about exceptional bundles, limits, or dedication projects to draw in new clients.

5. Building trust and providing high-quality services
Consultations before the service: Comprehend client requirements, inclinations, and expected aversions to

guarantee protected and compelling medicines.

Impressive skill and Dependability: Show up on time, keep a spotless and sterile climate, and convey successfully through the help.

Customized Consideration and Client Concentration: Focus on paying attention to client concerns, fitting administrations to their necessities, and surpassing assumptions.

Keep in mind, progress in locally established magnificence administrations requires steady development and a commitment to client fulfillment:

Remain Refreshed: Go to studios, online courses, or industry occasions to learn new procedures, patterns, and security conventions.

Put resources into Your Business: Think about proficient marking, promoting techniques, and systems administration chances to extend your compass and draw in new clients.

Center on Client Prosperity: Focus on security, cleanliness, and making an unwinding and spoiling experience for every client.

Keep in mind, each stroke of the brush, each layer of skincare, each many-sided nail plan, each loosening up knead is a demonstration of your abilities and the delight you bring to the universe of excellence. So, grab your tools, let your inner beauty guru shine, and let's get started on this beautiful journey of beautifying bodies, changing faces, and making the world feel more beautiful, one client at a time!

13. Plant Spread and Cultivating Administrations.

Do you have a green thumb? Transform your adoration for plants into a business by engendering and selling succulents, houseplants, or offering cultivating administrations like finishing or plant conferences for green-disapproved of people.

Ok, the enamoring universe of plant proliferation and cultivating! It doesn't matter if you're a seasoned gardener or just starting out as a botanist; cultivating your passion for caring for life can be extremely satisfying. We should investigate a rousing way of transforming your affection for plants into a satisfying and possibly productive endeavor:

1. Selling Engendered Plants:

Begin Little: Decide simple to-proliferate plants like succulents, spices, air plants, or normal houseplants to fabricate a different stock.

Ace Various Strategies: Investigate techniques like stem cuttings, division, layering, or joining to extend your engendering collection.

Events and markets in the area: Sell your engendered plants at ranchers markets, create fairs, spring up shops, or online commercial centers.

Discount Open doors: To provide your flourishing greenery to local cafes, offices, or plant stores, work together.

2.   Offering Plant Proliferation Administrations:

Taking care of Explicit Necessities: By providing services such as rooting cuttings, dividing clumps, or grafting unique varieties, you can assist fellow plant enthusiasts in propagating their beloved plants.

Workshops for Education: Share your insight by facilitating studios on plant engendering procedures, drawing on plant sweethearts and clients.

Custom Plant Spread Activities: Collaborate with people or organizations looking for explicit plants, offering customized spread administrations for special or interesting assortments.

Plant Kits and boxes to subscribe to: curate themed plant units with proliferated plants, care directions, and brightening components for a repetitive income stream.

3. Making Content and Building a Local area:

Drawing on Blog or Youtube Channel: Share your proliferation process, offer tips and instructional exercises, and motivate others with charming plant content.

Dynamic Virtual Entertainment Presence: Construct a local area of plant fans on stages like Instagram or Facebook, interface with clients, and feature your abilities.

Online Plant Counseling: Offer virtual interviews or interactive discussions, directing people on plant care, engendering difficulties, and picking the right vegetation for their spaces.

Partnerships and Collaborations: Collaborate with other plant-related organizations, powerhouses, or cultivating associations to grow your scope and crowd.

4. Broadening Your Plant-Based Business:
Plant Styling and Inside Plan: Offer home or office plant styling administrations, assisting clients curate wonderful indoor scenes with flourishing vegetation.
Terrariums and kits for DIY: Make pre-made or adaptable terrarium packs that incorporate proliferated plants, brightening components, and care directions.
Natural Plant Compost and Soil Blends: Create and sell your own natively constructed manure or soil blends took care of explicit plant needs and workable practices.

E-books and educational resources: Share your plant information through exhaustive digital books, online courses, or printable plant care guides.

Keep in mind, the outcome in the realm of plants requires devotion, tolerance, and a nonstop learning mentality:

Keep up to date: Find out about new plant patterns, research imaginative proliferation procedures, and remain informed about accepted procedures in plant care.

Fabricate Connections: Network with individual plant devotees, green experts, and expected clients to encourage a strong local area.

Natural Promotion: To align your business with environmental values, promote environmentally friendly products, responsible plant sourcing, and sustainable gardening methods.

Keep in mind, each fragile leaf spreading out, each energetic blossom decorating your space, each flourishing plant supported by your mastery, is a demonstration of your enthusiasm and the positive effect you bring to the universe of vegetation. In this way, snatch your planting gloves, let your plant engendering experiences start, and we should develop a flourishing business loaded up with life, magnificence, and the unending delights of developing things!

Keep in mind, outcome in any locally situated business require devotion, energy, and key preparation. Direct intensive statistical surveying, make a strong strategy, and influence your nearby local area while building areas of strength for a four qualities and dependability. With the right method and a hint of resourcefulness, you can transform your home into a center of enterprising achievement, encouraging satisfying work and monetary freedom. Sending off a locally situated business is a thrilling experience loaded up with potential, yet it likewise requires cautious preparation and commitment to make progress. Here are a few fundamental tips to direct you on your excursion:

Arranging and Arrangement:

Characterize your specialty and interest group: Distinguish an exceptional selling recommendation and comprehend who you're providing food your administrations successfully.

Foster a field-tested strategy: For direction, outline your objectives, strategies, financial projections, and marketing strategy.

Research lawful and administrative prerequisites: Guarantee you agree with nearby guidelines and get important allows and licenses.

Set up a committed work area: Make an agreeable and useful space for centered work and client cooperation.

Put resources into fundamental devices and innovation: Furnish yourself with the fundamental hardware and programming to meet your business needs.

Monetary Administration:

Track your costs and pay for tax and to track your progress, keep detailed records of all financial transactions.

Set cutthroat evaluating: Research market rates and calculate your expenses and offer to set fair and productive costs.

Think about protection: Investigate choices for responsibility protection and other inclusion to safeguard your business.

Foster a reserve funds and growth strategy: Dispense assets for future ventures, crises, and retirement to guarantee monetary strength.

Promoting and Marking:

Construct areas of strength for a presence: Make an expert site and dynamic virtual entertainment profiles to feature your administrations and interface with likely clients.

Make use of digital marketing devices: Influence Search engine optimization, email promoting, and internet publicizing to successfully arrive at your interest group.

Organization and assemble connections: Associate with different experts, likely accomplices, and clients in your field to grow your range and fabricate trust.

Foster a predictable brand personality: Make an unmistakable logo, slogan, and informing that mirrors your qualities and resounds with your crowd.

Client Concentration and Correspondence:

Convey remarkable client support: To build a loyal customer base, prioritize prompt communication, friendly interactions, and exceeding client expectations.

Collect feedback and change: effectively pay attention to client input and change your administrations and contributions to meet their advancing necessities.

Transparency and trust are built: Tell the truth and forthright about your administrations, costs, and arrangements to cultivate trust and long haul connections.

Offer different correspondence channels: To accommodate client preferences, provide options for in-person, phone, social media, and email communication.

Self-awareness and Improvement:

Keep awake to-date: Go to studios, online courses, and industry occasions to keep your abilities sharp and master recent fads.

Network with different business visionaries: Look for mentorship, share encounters, and gain from other people who have strolled the way before you.

Keep a good work-life balance: Put down stopping points, focus on taking care of oneself, and stay balanced to guarantee supportability and pleasure in your work.

Praise your accomplishments: Perceive your own advancement, appreciate your achievements, and remain roused for proceeding with progress.

Keep in mind, fabricating a fruitful locally established business takes time, exertion, and responsibility. By preparing, dealing with your funds successfully, promoting your administrations decisively, and focusing on client fulfillment, you can transform your enthusiasm into a flourishing endeavor that gives you pleasure and satisfaction.

Reward Tip: Don't be afraid to request help! For advice, funding, and opportunities to network, use online resources, government support programs, and local business organizations.

I'm here to be your virtual sidekick on this innovative excursion. Pose a particular inquiry you have about executing these tips, beating difficulties, or calibrating your locally established business technique. Together, we should transform your fantasies into the real world and construct a fruitful endeavor that flourishes!

Conclusion

The universe of locally established organizations is overflowing with invigorating conceivable outcomes, offering an opportunity to transform your enthusiasm and abilities into a satisfying endeavor. Whether you're attracted to the active fulfillment of home improvement, the imaginative appeal of music examples, or the sensitive creativity of plant spread, the way to progress lies in cautious preparation, commitment, and an emphasis on conveying extraordinary worth to your clients.

Keep in mind that your journey will not be without obstacles. From exploring lawful prerequisites to dominating new abilities to finding the ideal balance between fun and serious activities, there will be knocks along the street. With each obstacle to survive, you'll learn, develop, and fabricate a business that mirrors your special vision and gives pleasure to both you and your clients.

Therefore, take pleasure in the excitement of this business venture! Furnish yourself with the fundamental tips and direction gave, tap into your boundless potential, and set out on an excursion of building a flourishing locally established business that satisfies your fantasies and makes an enduring imprint on your picked field.

Or more all, never neglect to focus on the energy that energized this endeavor. Allow your energy to radiate through in each connection, each help conveyed, and each deterrent survives. For it is with immovable commitment and a feeling of development that you'll fabricate a fruitful business, yet additionally cut your own exceptional way in the realm of locally situated business people.

You are in control of the future. Go forward, overcome the difficulties, and make your business dreams a reality!